GWR REFLECTIONS

A COLLECTION OF PHOTOGRAPHS FROM THE BBC HULTON PICTURE LIBRARY

BY

KEITH BECK & NIGEL HARRIS

Silver Link Publishing Ltd

The Coach House, Garstang Road, St. Michaels, Lancashire PR3 0TG·

CONTENTS

ACKNOWLEDGEMENTS

AS with the two previous volumes in this series, *LNER Reflections* and *LMS Reflections*, this book has been compiled exclusively from the extensive and wide-ranging archives of the BBC Hulton Picture Library. Once again, thanks are due to the many individuals who gave freely of their assistance and advice, for which SLP is sincerely grateful.

Thanks first of all to Janet Andrew, Head of BBC Data Services & Sales, BBC Hulton Picture Library Acting Manager Bob Bright and BBC Data Marketing Manager Peter Elliott for their valued comments and advice at every stage. We would also like to express our sincere appreciation to Hulton Picture Library Deputy Manager Roger Wemyss-Brooks and the always-helpful Picture Assistants for their advice and guidance regarding the Library's complex filing system and layout. Their help has resulted in the 'unearthing' of some extremely interesting pictures of great historical importance. A special word of thanks also for Negative Assistant Matthew Butson, for sifting out the relevant negatives and also Picture Assistant Sue Wookey, who collated all available caption material from the HPL's files.

SLP would also like to thank Ray Towell, Engineering Assistant to the Chief Mechanical Engineer, at the National Railway Museum, York, and also John Edgington, of the NRM Library, for their assistance with detailed historical information for some of the photographs. Thanks are also due to Derek Mercer for producing first-rate prints from the original negatives, and producing superb copy negatives, where required.

Finally, we would like to express our most sincere thanks to GWR historian Keith Beck, for grouping these photographs into an interesting sequence, and for providing such absorbing captions and text.

FRONT COVER: The 'King' 4—6—0, introduced by C.B. Collett in 1927, gave the GWR Britain's most powerful passenger locomotive, and the class represented the ultimate development of the Churchward four-cylinder 4—6—0, first introduced in 1907 with the famous 'Star' class, which itself served until the 1950s. The 'Kings' were thoroughly majestic in appearance and performance, as illustrated in this impressive study of No. 6029 *King Edward VIII*, making haste near Old Oak Common on May 22 1936. Formerly named *King Stephen*, this was No. 6029's first revenue-earning run after being renamed following the death of King George V and the succession of the new monarch. Although Edward VIII abdicated in December 1936, No. 6029 retained his royal name until withdrawal in July 1962.

REAR COVER: Until the opening of the British Railway's Locomotive Testing Station at Rugby on October 19 1948, the only stationary locomotive test plant in this country was located at the GWR's Swindon works. Pictured here at high speed on the Swindon 'rolling road' on January 26 1932 is 'Castle' No. 4009 *Shooting Star*; an impressive spectacle.

PREVIOUS PAGE: A classic image of 'top link' GWR steam at Paddington in the first quarter of the 20th century: in June 1923 'Star' 4—6—0 No. 4049 *Princess Maud* makes a vigorous departure, typical of Churchward's engines, its carriages newly repainted in the chocolate and cream livery re-introduced that year. As a legacy of the war years No. 4049 is unlined, but full lining-out for express engines was to reappear on No. 4073 *Caerphilly Castle* two months later. Note the upper quadrant advanced starting signal: this electrically operated semaphore had three positions, as were popular on American railways — horizontal for 'Stop', inclined upwards at 45 degrees for 'Caution' and vertically upright for 'clear'. The GWR was among the first in Britain to experiment with signals showing more than two aspects.

Typeset by Lloyd Williams, Southport and printed in the United Kingdom by Netherwood Dalton & Co. Ltd., Huddersfield, Yorkshire.

Designed by Nigel Harris.
Front Cover design by Phil Cousins.

GWR reflections: a collection of photographs
  from the BBC Hulton Picture Library.
1. Great Western Railway - History -
Pictorial works
I. Beck, Keith M. II. Harris, Nigel
III. BBC Hulton Picture Library
385'.0942 HE3020.G8
ISBN 0-947971-13-0

Above: A fascinating view of Brunel's Royal Albert Bridge, over the Tamar at Saltash, on July 18 1938 as 2—6—2T No. 4598 of Laira shed crosses the bridge at the head of an up local goods train. The majority of the GWR's small 2—6—2Ts of the '4500' and '4575' classes (the latter having larger, higher tanks) were always to be found in the West Country. Built in April 1927, No. 4598 spent its entire life working in Devon and Cornwall until withdrawal in December 1956. At the time this photograph was taken, the bridge (opened in 1859) was being painted grey at the request of the Air Raid Precaution authorities, in anticipation of the war which broke out on September 3 1939.

FOREWORD
by
DAVID SHEPHERD OBE, FRSA

IF the best bedroom in a house in North London fills with smoke every time the people who live there now light a fire in the fireplace, I can tell them why. I spent all my early childhood in that house and my father was a railway fanatic. He built a magnificent 'O' gauge layout and, in order to create a more realistic curve between London and the terminus at the other side of the room, he bored a hole right through the chimney breast. It seems that model railway enthusiasts will go to almost any lengths to achieve realism! So was nurtured from the very beginning my passion for steam railways, though I would never have dreamed then that I would become involved to the extent I now have, owning two ex-British Rail main line steam locomotives, BR Standard Class 4MT 4—6—0 No. 75029 *The Green Knight*, and Standard Class 9F 2—10—0 No. 92203 *Black Prince*, and they were both built at Swindon, home of the GWR.

I was delighted when I was invited to write the foreword to the third volume in this splendid series of 'Reflections'. I think nostalgia and appreciation and an awareness of an age gone for ever is important, for it gives an extra dimension to our daily lives. So much has been swept away in the name of that ugly word, progress.

All the books in this series, illustrated entirely from the archives of the BBC Hulton Picture Library, remind us of the heroic days of steam when 'Castles' and 'Kings' and the great engines of the other railways in the pre-grouping era, were part of the daily scene. I believe the designer of those masterpieces was not only a mechanical engineer, making sure that his creation did the job for which it was intended; he was an artist as well and he made it 'look right', a sad contrast indeed to the age in which we now live when the latter point seems to have been forgotten altogether. Built-in obsolescence is the norm now and we are all the poorer for it.

Where I believe these books do such a great service is in reminding us not only of the mighty locomotives, but also of all the detail that went into making up the pattern and complex-

ity of a living steam railway. We owe so much to the BBC Hulton Picture Library. For example, men had pride in their railway in those days as shown in the photograph of a team of dedicated workers polishing a trio of magnificent 'King' class locomotives, ready to go out on the road from Swindon depot, until they shone. What memories are evoked by photographs of wives and sweethearts saying goodbye to their soldier husbands and boyfriends about to depart for World War II battle zones, possibly never to return. We can almost hear the stirring theme of Rachmaninov's Second Piano Concerto which accompanied Celia Johnson saying goodbye to Trevor Howard in the film 'Brief Encounter' on the smoke-filled platform. This is the very stuff of nostalgia. This book reminds us of the splendid 'characters' who worked for the railways in days past: why don't railway inspectors look like some of the splendid gentlemen illustrated in these pages any more?

The railway preservationists in the

last twenty years, of which I am proud to have been one, have done a great deal to keep alive just a tiny part of Britain's great steam era which, instead of going out in a blaze of glory in the summer of 1968, went out in a scene of total degradation. Today, we can give footplate rides on living steam locomotives, but only the historic photograph can cover the whole emotional scene, and this series of books amply fulfils this purpose.

David Shepherd

INTRODUCTION

THE GWR was a truly remarkable railway; indeed it may justifiably be claimed that in the course of its 112 years of life it became more than simply a railway, developing into a proud institution with its own high standards and traditions. Unlike any of the other British railway companies, the GWR retained its original name through the Grouping of 1923 when it simply absorbed 16 minor railway companies, all but three in South Wales, and it was the only company to celebrate its centenary, in 1935. However, one of the best known characteristics of this much-loved railway was that from its birth to its lamented passing, at Nationalisation in 1948, the GWR succeeded in unique style always to be 'different'.

From the very beginning, it stood apart from the other main lines of this country by being constructed to the 7ft ¼in so-called broad gauge, as a consequence of the vision and seemingly boundless imagination of its great Engineer, Isambard Kingdom Brunel. The 'baulk' road of the broad gauge track, its disc-and-crossbar

signals and other unique features combined to create what Brunel not immodestly described as "the greatest work in England". Furthermore, this flamboyant attitude was accompanied by the breath-taking concept that the GWR should be merely the first link in a chain of transport linking London with New York: the Great Western Railway was to be extended across the vastness of the Atlantic Ocean by means of the Great Western Steamship Company!

Within 20 years or so of its incorporation, in 1835, the GWR embraced two gauges, for in addition to its own broad gauge system it had, through amalgamation, inherited the 4ft 8½in gauge routes of the Shrewsbury & Birmingham and Shrewsbury & Chester Railways, and it was to continue in this unusual situation for nearly 40 years. The GWR's history at this time is one of virtually continuous amalgamation with so-called 'narrow gauge' lines, accompanied by the gradual conversion of its original broad gauge lines to mixed gauge routes, by the addition of

Above: The broad gauge in all its glory! Dean 4—2—2 *Great Western* of the 'Rover' class (as the renewals of the 'Iron Dukes' were commonly known) was built in May 1888 as a replacement of the very first 8ft 'Single', which had been built as a 2—2—2 in April 1846 and altered to a 4—2—2 a few months later. As the 1846 locomotive had been withdrawn as early as December 1870 there was no way in which the new engine could be regarded as being a 'renewal'! It was the penultimate broad gauge engine built, the very last being *Tornado*, which entered service in July of the same year. *Great Western* is seen here on a down express at Didcot, around 1890, the building in the background being the old engine shed which was opened as a mixed gauge depot in 1857. The boys standing on the platform highlight the large proportions of the beautifully clean locomotive — and note the neatly trimmed coal, with large 'cobs' stacked carefully around the edges of the tender.

a third rail to each track, or by genuine narrowing to standard gauge, as the 4ft 8½in tracks had become known. However, in 1876 the GWR took over the working of the hitherto independent companies routes west of Bristol and it consequently reacquired a considerable mileage of broad gauge railway, all west of Exeter, together with a large amount of broad gauge locomotives and rolling stock, to swell its own diminishing tally. Not until May 1892, 54 years after the opening of its first length of line, was the GWR to be wholly 'in step' with the rest of the main line British railway system, at least as far as gauge was concerned.

The initials GWR, according to unkind critics (of whom there were many!) meant the 'Great Way Round' in recognition of the company's rather circuitous main lines: the route to the West of England was via the original main line between London and Bristol; passengers to and from South Wales travelled via Gloucester, while the main line to Birmingham and the North was via Reading and Oxford. In 1886, the Company opened its new route to South Wales, via the Severn Tunnel, which was one of the most difficult railway projects ever undertaken in this country and by far the greatest and most costly work ever accomplished by one company. Later, between 1900 and 1911, new and more direct lines were opened: to the West of England, via Westbury; to South Wales via Badminton (thus avoiding Bristol); in West Wales to a new harbour for Irish traffic, at Fishguard, and to Banbury, Birmingham and the North, via Bicester. Once again, no other British railway company ever undertook such a vast and expensive programme of new works.

Brunel's broad gauge had ensured that GWR locomotives of the early days were very different from those constructed by other companies, and the more liberal dimensions made possible by the wider gauge ensured that Daniel Gooch's magnificent 8ft 'Singles' were by far the most powerful and speedy engines in the kingdom. At the same time, the greater width of the carriages provided accommodation which was generally superior to that provided elsewhere on the 'narrow gauge' routes. Also, for many years, the GWR enjoyed the distinction of running the fastest train in the world — the 'Exeter Express' as it was first known. However, the advantages afforded by the broad gauge became liabilities within a few years as it became increasingly apparent that its days were numbered in view of the widescale adoption elsewhere of the standard gauge — or 'colliery gauge' as Brunel dismissively described it. Unfortunately, as a result of this

Above: Collett 'Castle' 4—6—0 No.5006 *Tregenna Castle* **leaves Paddington in charge of the 9.45am train to Gloucester on June 6 1932. This was the outward working of the famous 'Cheltenham Flyer', the 'World's Fastest Train', and the return journey was to be a world record run: the 77.3 miles from Swindon to Paddington were covered in 56 min 47 sec at an average speed of 81.6 mph, 70 miles being run at an average speed of 87.5 mph, with a maximum speed of 92 mph. Introduced in 1923, 'Castles' were still being built by British Railways at Swindon in 1950!**

attitude, there was little development in locomotive design on that gauge with the consequence that even in 1892, the main West of England express services were still hauled by engines whose basic design dated back to the 1840s!

Just as the advent of the 20th century witnessed the construction and opening of the great 'cut-offs' which created the new main lines mentioned earlier, so in the realm of locomotive engineering the genius of George Jackson Churchward, appointed as Chief Mechanical Engineer in 1902, created a family of standard locomotives, all fitted with tapered,

domeless Belpaire boilers and outside cylinders which all had a great deal in common with each other — but little or nothing in common with locomotives found on other British systems. The basic principles of design embodied in Churchward's locomotives were to remain unchanged for the remainder of the GWR's existence, with the result that the last Swindon designs were essentially modernised versions of the prototypes introduced over the previous 40 years. Alone amongst the 'Big Four' companies after the Grouping, the GWR retained right-hand drive for all its locomotives, thus ensuring another distinguishing feature for the GWR, compared with its contemporaries.

The unique disc-and-crossbar signals which were a feature of the broad gauge lines were gradually replaced from 1869 onwards by the more usual semaphores, and by the 1890s all the Brunel signalling had gone. However, even here the GWR remained 'out of step' for in contrast to the upper quadrant signals adopted widely elsewhere, it adopted lower quadrant operation which it retained until the end of its life. Even when electrifying the signalling on the approaches to Paddington, the GWR did not conform to what was evolving as the standard multi-aspect colour light indications: the GWR's new colour light signals gave the same indications as those of the semaphores they replaced. In the use of its Automatic Train Control system (ATC) adopted as part of main line signalling, the GWR was 50 years ahead of the rest of the British railway system and this undoubtedly contributed to another important 'difference' — that of comparative immunity from

serious accidents compared with the unenviable record of some other companies, not least the LMS.

GWR 'firsts' which set the Company apart included the introduction of the first diesel railcars, the first railway-owned air services, the now-universal use of train reporting numbers, the first stationary test plant for locomotives in Britain, at Swindon works, the early introduction of numerous, vacuum-brake fitted express goods trains, and the first motor-rail trains (through the Severn Tunnel). The Company, as the GWR was always known to its staff, also built the longest and widest carriages ever to run in this country, and also the marvellous Super Saloons, comfortable and splendid vehicles named after members of the Royal Family. For many years the GWR held the record for the world's longest non-stop run with 'The Cornish Riviera' express and for some years during the 1930s it regained the distinction (held twice previously during the 19th century) for operating the world's

fastest train — the famous 'Cheltenham Flyer'.

Finally, 'God's Wonderful Railway', as the Company was affectionately known by its devotees, proved to be well-nigh indestructible, despite Nationalisation and some determined efforts to ensure its demise. In many ways, British Railways (Western Region) was "but Great Western, writ large" for many years. Even today, 40 years later, Churchward and Collett locomotives with copper-capped chimneys and painted in Brunswick green livery can still be seen and heard, hauling trains of chocolate and cream liveried carriages. Swindon works, alas, may be no more, but the characteristic 'Swindon sound' may still be heard. Together with this collection of superb photographs drawn from the archives of the BBC Hulton Picture Library, they help enable young and old alike to share in these evocative 'reflections' of the GWR.

Keith M. Beck

Above: Collett 4—6—0 No.6000 *King George V* **takes 'The Cornish Riviera Express' out of Paddington on the occasion of this famous train's jubilee — July 8 1929. Two complete sets of new carriages were built at Swindon to mark the occasion, and at 9ft 7in wide these splendid GWR passenger vehicles were the widest carriages to run on** any British Railway — made possible by the generous clearances which were a legacy of the broad gauge. The 30 'King' class engines constructed between 1927 and 1930 remained as the most powerful express passenger locomotives of GWR origin for the remainder of the Company's existence.

PADDINGTON

BRUNEL'S STATION

PADDINGTON was synonymous with the GWR: not only was it the Company's seat of government with the Directors and the General Manager exercising authority from within its walls, but it was also the 'Alpha and the Omega', the beginning and the ending, for the majority of the Company's express passenger services. For Torquay and Penzance; for Cardiff, Swansea and Fishguard (for the South of Ireland); for Birmingham, Wolverhampton, Birkenhead and North Wales; for Weymouth and the Channel Islands; and, above all, for Bristol, Paddington was *the* station. Moreover, as with so much else on the GWR — the broad gauge, the Royal Albert Bridge, Box Tunnel, the timber viaducts — Paddington was very much Brunel's creation and legacy. Essentially unchanged and unchanging in spirit, despite successive alterations and extensions — and even a change of gauge — Paddington was, and still is, Brunel's Paddington.

Above all, Paddington had been the site of the London terminus of the GWR from its first days: only the old Euston (long since destroyed by an act of official vandalism) could rival Paddington. However, the Paddington known to generations of GWR passengers, and still familiar today, did not exist when the first passengers were carried on the newly-opened GWR. The original station, constructed on the same site, was intended to be only a temporary structure pending the construction of a permanent and much finer set of premises, though it eventually served for no less than 16 years before being replaced by the present station.

The departure side of the terminus, was brought into use on January 16, 1854, when the roof and the arrival side were still far from complete. It was little wonder that Brunel re-

Above: Paddington in July 1912. Special trains for the Royal Garden Party at Windsor stand at No.4 and No.5 platforms, two of Churchward's famous 'Star' class 4—6—0s, Nos.4023 *King George* **(left) and 4003** *Lode Star* **having brought the trains into the station. Two of the more usual carriage pilots, Wolverhampton-built 0—6—0STs of the '850' class, are in the background. Crimson lake had just replaced the overall brown carriage livery introduced by the GWR in 1908 in place of the familiar chocolate and cream (though GWR carriages had been painted in overall brown livery prior to 1864). Both 'Stars' were long-lived engines: No. 4003 was not withdrawn until July 1951, and No. 4023 lasted exactly a year longer — both were withdrawn from Landore (Swansea). No. 4023 was renamed** *Danish Monarch* **in 1927 (following introduction of Collett's 'King' 4—6—0s) but the name was removed in 1940; while** *Lode Star* **is still with us, at the GWR Museum, in Swindon.**

Left: The last day of the broad gauge. The 10.15am 'Cornishman' of May 20 1892, the last broad gauge train to Penzance, leaves Paddington, hauled by 4—2—2 *Great Western* — only four years old, but destined for the scrapyard. At No.2 platform, a 'narrow gauge' 7ft 'Single' of either the 'Queen' or '157' classes stands at the head of what from May 21 will be a 'standard gauge' train — even on the GWR.

Above: 20 years later in October 1912, one of Churchward's two-cylinder 4—6—0s, No.2928 *St. Sebastian,* leaves Paddington on a Bath Spa and Bristol express. The first carriage is a Churchward 'Concertina' — so nick-named because of the inset doors. The small 'star' motif on the smokebox door suggests that this engine has been shedded at Wolverhampton, Stafford Road, as for many years this was a regular 'trade mark' of that shed. No.2928 (built September 1907) was another long-lived engine which remained at work (latterly from Westbury) until August 1948. On the left is a train of close-coupled four-wheeled suburban stock, typical of the London and Birmingham suburban trains of that time; on the right in the bay behind the 'A' Excursion Platform (an extension of No.1 Platform(are two bogie clerestory carriages.

corded: "the difficulties of proceeding successively with different portions of the new work on the site of the old buildings without interfering too much with the carrying of the traffic in a station, already far too small for the wants, have been very great". On May 29 the arrival platforms were opened, and by the following February the work was completed, apart from painting. It is a tribute to Brunel's foresight that this station of 1854 proved sufficient for the GWR's traffic, without needing to be enlarged (apart from replacing carriage sidings by three additional platforms in 1878, 1884 and 1893 respectively) for nearly 60 years. Paddington was one of the first places in London to be illuminated by electricity, this being inaugurted at Christmas 1880.

9

Above: Churchward 'Star' 4—6—0 No.4021
King Edward (of Old Oak Common shed)
stands at No.2 platform at the head of the
5.00pm Paddington—Cheltenham Spa express
in July 1923. The copper-capped chimney and
brass safety-valve cover have been painted
over, while the brass beading was removed
from the splashers during the war years, and
was never replaced. Less than a month later
the 'Stars' were no longer the most powerful
express passenger engines on the GWR, for
Caerphilly Castle was already nearing
completion in Swindon Works. In common
with the other Stars named after Kings
No.4021 was renamed in 1927: as *British
Monarch* it was the only example to retain its
name when the surviving 'Monarchs' had
their names removed during the Second
World War. No.4021 was withdrawn in
October 1952, from Oxford.

Above: 'Castle' 4—6—0 No.5004 *Llanstephan Castle*
approaches Paddington on July 13 1937, at the end of
its non-stop run from Swindon on the 'Cheltenham
Flyer' at an average speed of 71.4 mph. Ranelagh
Bridge locomotive servicing sidings, with their
typical GWR water tower, is on the left. No.5004
spent much of its life working from Old Oak Common
shed, and was withdrawn in April 1962.

Left: The exterior of Paddington station, on August 9
1929, showing the departure side facing Eastbourne
Terrace (left). The Great Western Royal Hotel (right)
was opened on June 9 1854 and leased to a company
formed for the purpose by some of the GWR's officers
and shareholders. Brunel was amongst the Directors
of the Hotel Company and soon became its Chairman.
It was not until 1896 that the GWR took over the
running of the premises.

Left: The arrival side at Paddington, on August 9 1929. The great arched roof (right) was not part of Brunel's original station, but was added in 1913 when additional platforms were also provided — making a total of 12. An impressive array of posters on the left promote the GWR's new 'Cambrian Coast Express', half day excursions to Swindon (return fare 5 shillings!) new through services to the Continent, courtesy of the GWR and SR, and holidays in the Isle of Man and Ireland.

Left, below: The interior of Brunel's station, as newly opened in 1854. The arrival platforms are on the right, with three platform faces serving only two lines; the central space between the two island platforms is occupied by carriage sidings (replaced between 1878 and 1893 by three additional platforms) while the departure side (left) is served by three lines and three platform faces. The arches below the scrollwork of the great iron and glass screens are those of the old Bishop's Road Bridge. (From a contemporary engraving).

Paddington was, of course, originally a broad gauge station; however, the 'narrow gauge' had invaded in 1861 to provide a means for through services to and from north of Wolverhampton and over the West Midland's lines from Oxford to Worcester, Wolverhampton and Hereford. Successive conversions of the Weymouth, South Wales and Hereford (via Gloucester) lines to the 'narrow gauge' meant that from 1872 the only broad-gauge trains still using the station were those between Paddington and the West of England, apart from one or two Windsor and Reading 'locals'. By 1878, the only remaining broad-gauge services were the Bristol and West of England trains and one train from Windsor, the 9.05am, which remained for the benefit of the Company Chairman, Sir Daniel Gooch, who travelled up to Paddington. He returned to Windsor every evening by means of a slip carriage from a Bristol train until 1883, when the Windsor branch was 'narrowed' to standard gauge. After 1883, the only remaining broad-gauge trains were those between Paddington and the West of England.

Finally, on May 20, 1892, the dreadful day came when even that last bastion of the 'true gauge' fell to the assault of what had once been dismissed by Daniel Gooch as the "coal cart gauge". It was, perhaps, a kindness that he did not live to see that day when the last train on the broad gauge left Paddington station behind one of his magnificent 8ft 'Singles', which for over 40 years had been the premier express engines and almost part of Paddington itself. Brunel had not even seen the invasion into his beloved station of the 'narrow gauge' rails, having died in 1859, two years prior to that ominous event.

Above: The platform bridge in use between No.3 and No.4 platforms, circa 1910. A similar bridge was provided between No.1 and No.2 platforms, their purpose being to facilitate easy access for the benefit of mail and newspaper traffic. The train at No.7 platform is formed of close-coupled stock for the Paddington suburban services, whilst a carriage truck, carrying the load for which such vehicles were intended, stands alongside No.5 platform.

Right: The station interior at Paddington, during the 1920s, seen from the roof arches above No. 3 platform. A notable feature of Brunel's roof was the provision of two 'transepts' in each of the three arched roof sections, which thus resembled the nave and side aisles of a great church. The 'transepts' not only provided additional light, but also cross-bracing for the whole roof structure. Pictures like this highlight the wide range of rolling stock (not to mention road vehicles!) which could be seen at Paddington in the middle and late 1920s. The train set beyond the taxis consists of (on the left) a 57ft bow-ended third class vehicle, of a design built in seven Lots, to diagram C54, in the period 1926-1929, whilst the two right-hand vehicles are corridor third class carriages of 1925, of Lot 1374. The three clerestory-roofed coaches in the centre are 46ft non-corridor 'all-thirds', of a design introduced in 1894. The vehicle in the foreground is a 'brake third' of 1929, built as part of Lot 1427.

Left: Cleaning the glass in the roof was a major undertaking, involving erecting extensive scaffolding. High up beneath the central roof span, a workman fixes a scaffold pole in position at 11.34am on October 13 1930, while far below, the suburban train headed by one of Churchward's 'County Tanks' looks as if it belongs on a model railway! The original Topical Press caption records: "Workmen are now busily engaged in cleaning and renovating the second of the four roof spans at Paddington station. This will take them four months, during which time 40 gallons of Hydroflouric will be used to remove 4½ tons of soot. 6,000 panes of glass will have to be cleaned inside and out, and 139 cwts of paint, 300 gallons of tar, 50 gallons of turps and 20 gallons of linseed oil will be used in renovation."

Left: The exterior of the roof, also on October 13 1930, as the workmen enjoy a lofty lunch on the very edge of the towering main arched span. The old Departure Signal Box can be seen on No.2 platform, just below Bishop's Road Bridge: this signal box was demolished when the platforms were extended during the 1931 modernisation scheme.

Below: An evocative period scene at Paddington in May 1911, which vividly conjures the atmosphere at the GWR's London terminus in the immediate Pre-First World War years. On the right, one of Churchward's famous 'City' class double-framed 4—4—0s stands at No.9 platform. There were only 20 'Cities', half of them being rebuilds from the earlier 'Atbara' class, which had carried smaller boilers. In the foreground is a luggage pen from which passengers are claiming cases and cabin trunks for loading onto the waiting 'cabs', the majority of which are horse-drawn vehicles. The heavy luggage is explained by the fact that the train just visible (left) is the newly-arrived 'Boston Boat Train', conveying American tourists.

Right: An image of privilege at Paddington as Eton scholars arrive at the end of the summer term, in July 1923. This was somewhat ironic, for there had been implacable opposition by the Provost and Fellows of Eton College to the construction of the GWR, which had resulted in a special section in the Act of Incorporation: "No diversion, branch, or station, is to be made within three miles of Eton College, and the Company is to maintain a sufficient additional number of persons for the purpose of preventing or restricting access to the said railway by Scholars of Eton College aforesaid whether on the Foundation or otherwise, such persons to be under the orders of the Provost and Head Master". The smock-coated railwayman enjoying his cigarette and surveying the scene in the background provides a sharp contrast to the wing-collars, white gloves, spats and top hats of the GWR's patrons!

Above: A Paddington departure during the railwaymen's strike of 1919 as Churchward 'Star' 4—6—0 No.4004 *Morning Star* leaves the station with a Plymouth-bound train. The 'Stars' (introduced in 1907) were the foremost front-line passenger locomotives of the pre and immediate post-war years of the early 20th Century, and established the trend for four-cylinder 4—6—0 construction at Swindon which lasted into the 1950s, when British Railways was still building 'Castle' 4—6—0s, virtually to their original 1923 diagrams! In this picture, although the 'Star' is very clean, the legacy of the wartime years is still apparent — the copper chimney cap and brass safety valve 'bonnet' are both painted austerely, in black.

Above: 1924 brought another railway strike, that of the footplatemen members of ASLEF, which began on January 24. In this unusual view of Paddington, crowded with carriages but otherwise almost deserted, a handful of passengers are dimly visible, waiting in hope on Platform 1, on the extreme left. On the right is 'Bulldog' class double-framed 4—4—0 No.3300, formerly named *Pendennis Castle*, a name by this stage carried by one of the new 'Castles', No.4079. A total of 156 of the 5ft 8in-wheeled 'Bulldogs' were built between 1899 and 1910, the first 20 (including No.3300) having been rebuilt from the earlier 'Duke' class, which had domed boilers. The 'Bulldogs' lasted much longer than the express passenger 4—4—0s, the last two survivors not being withdrawn until 1951.

Left: In this sharply contrasting view of Paddington, also during the 1924 strike, No.1 platform is thronged with would-be passengers. Only a handful of the prospective travellers are women — among them a nurse — and all the gentlemen are wearing hats of some description, from flat caps to bowlers!

Right: The holiday exodus at Paddington on July 14 1928. The train at No. 1 platform is not, for once, 'The Limited'. The rear carriage, a Churchward 'Toplight', carries destination boards which read: "Paddington & Aberystwyth via Carmarthen" — a service first introduced at the turn of the century, but later overshadowed by the Cambrian Railways' route. The carriage pilot is one of the small 2—6—2Ts of the '4500' class, previously confined to the West of England and Monmouthshire Valleys branches, which had recently arrived at Old Oak Common to provide more powerful motive power for the Paddington empty stock workings. A tell-tale wisp of steam from the blistershaped cover on the front corner of the firebox indicates that the handhole beneath is incorrectly seated, and 'blowing'. Once again, the picture emphasises that hats of all kinds were very much in fashion!

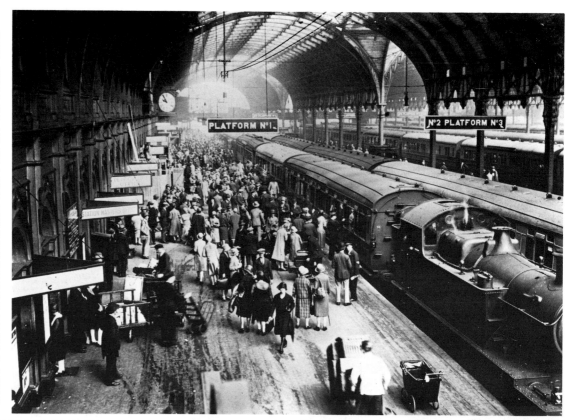

Above: A very distinguished company servant — the Chief Station Master at Paddington, Mr. James Page, at his desk in January 1926, on the occasion of his retirement after 50 years service with the GWR.

Right: A detailed view of the well-known clock above No.1 platform, on July 21 1931. Made by Kays, of Worcester, this replaced an earlier clock situated further along the platform. When first erected (during the first decade of this century) there was elaborate scroll-work above each of the three clock faces, but this was subsequently removed.

BRUNEL'S BROAD GAUGE

ISAMBARD Kingdom Brunel (1806-1859) was the creator of the GWR, which he justly claimed was "the finest work in England". Not only were Paddington and the main line to Bristol his work, but the 7ft metals of the broad gauge laid on longitudinal timbers and known as the 'baulk road', set the GWR apart from all other railways, as did the unique disc-and-crossbar signals. Responsible also for the Bristol & Exeter, South Devon, Cornwall and South Wales Railways (all broad gauge) Brunel's greatest engineering triumph was probably the Royal Albert Bridge which carried the baulk road into Cornwall. His fertile and imaginative genius also resulted in the adoption of the 'Atmospheric System' on the South Devon Railway, where a pipe was laid between the rails into which a projection from the train passed, via a longitudinal slot. Air was pumped out of the pipe at the destination, and the vacuum formed inside the pipe drew the train along the rails. The longitudinal slot was made airtight through the use of heavily greased leather flaps, but the grease proved irresistible to rats, which chewed the flaps, making them incapable of maintaining an airtight seal, and the system eventually proved unworkable. The failure of this form of traction, in favour of conventional locomotives, left a legacy of severe gradients and curves as a lasting frustration for the motive power department of the GWR. Brunel's broad gauge enabled the operation of fast, comfortable and very stable trains, but the adoption throughout the remainder of the country of 4ft 8½in as the standard gauge left the GWR isolated, and the broad gauge was finally abolished in 1892.

Left: Isambard Kingdom Brunel — the GWR's brilliant engineer, with characteristic cigar and top hat.

Above: Watched by a bowler-hatted gentleman in the foreground (the photographer's assistant, perhaps?), a Gooch 4—2—2 of the 'Rover' class of 26 examples, hurries past with a GWR express whose first vehicle appears to be a full brake of either Lot 255 or 258, of May 1882, built in the number series 134-142. These vehicles were 40ft in length, 10ft wide and 16 tons 1 cwt in weight (tare).

Facing page: Brunel was also responsible for the recruitment to the GWR of Daniel Gooch, who was only 21 years of age when appointed Locomotive Superintendent in April 1837. During his 27-year tenure of that office, until he resigned in October 1864, he was responsible for the design and construction of the majority of the GWR's broad gauge locomotives, some of which were still in service in 1892. He also designed the first locomotives for three other broad gauge lines, the Bristol & Exeter, the South Devon and the Vale of Neath Railways — his influence was therefore considerable. Gooch resigned as Locomotive Superintendent in order to supervise the laying of the first trans-Atlantic telegraph cable, using his friend Brunel's great steamship, the *Great Eastern.* This was unsuccessful at the first attempt, so a second attempt was made in June 1866 and on July 27 Gooch had the satisfaction of sending the first telegram from America to Ireland. For accomplishing this great work Gooch was made a baronet.

In the interval between the two expeditions to attempt the laying of the trans-Atlantic cable, Gooch had become the Chairman of his old company, which had run into very considerable financial difficulties. The Directors had decided that he was the only man who could restore the GWR to its former health, but Gooch was not even a Director. However, by virtue of certain provisions of the Amalgamation Acts of 1854 and 1863 (the former being concerned with the amalgamation of the two 'Shrewsbury' companies, the Shrewsbury & Chester and the Shrewsbury & Birmingham, and the latter with amalgamation of the West Midland Railway) Sir Watkin Wynn had the right to be a Director or to nominate someone to take his place, and he duly resigned and nominated Gooch to represent him! Gooch was soon elected in his own right.

Daniel Gooch MP, as he had also become, having been elected to represent the Cricklade Division of Wiltshire (though he never once spoke in the House of Commons during his 20 years membership!) faced a tremendous task in restoring the financial viability of the GWR, but with his firm leadership and prudent management this was accomplished. By 1872 the GWR was able to contemplate undertaking the colossal task of constructing the Severn Tunnel which was to cost nearly £2 million! On October 15 1889 'Good Sir Daniel', as he was widely known, died after a long illness. Of his 73 years, 51 had been devoted to the GWR; 27 years as Locomotive Superintendent and then, after a year's interval, a further 24 as Chairman. As well as designing and building locomotives of far greater power and speed than any others in the country, and then rescuing the Company from the verge of insolvency and establishing it on a firm and prosperous basis, he was also the founder of Swindon Works and the town of New Swindon, and the man whose perseverance ensured the construction of the Severn Tunnel. Whilst Brunel's name is very well known for his role in constructing the GWR, the role and contribution of Sir Daniel Gooch in subsequent years were of equally crucial importance.

Above: Gooch 8ft 'Single' *Perseus* in original condition, at Paddington in 1852. A total of 30 examples were built between 1846 and 1855, and the type served as the GWR's premier express passenger engines until the end of the broad gauge. However, individual engines did not run throughout the period, as from 1871 the majority of the 'Iron Dukes' were replaced by new engines carrying the same names (broad gauge engines of GWR origin had names only and were never numbered) and these were officially described as 'renewals' or 'rebuilds'. The last of the original engines, *Estaffete*, was withdrawn in December 1885. They were capable of an impressive turn of speed, and on May 14 1848, *Great Britain* ran from Paddington to Didcot (53 miles) in 47 minutes, at an average start-to-stop speed of 67½mph. Michael Almond was *Great Britain's* regular driver, with Richard Denham as his fireman.

Left: The broad gauge was carried westwards from Bristol by the Bristol & Exeter Railway whose engines, unlike those on the GWR, were numbered but not named. No.71 was a 4—4—0ST designed by James Pearson and built by the Vulcan Foundry in July 1867. From 1876, when the GWR took over the working of the BER and the other lines in the West of England, this engine became No.2044: it was withdrawn in December 1882.

Above: Further west, on the former Bristol & Exeter Railway main line, the 'Flying Dutchman' is seen near Bridgwater, running over the mixed-gauge 'baulk road', circa 1885, with the inevitable 8ft 'Single' in charge. The third rail creating the mixed gauge had reached Bristol by June 1874 and was then extended westwards to Exeter by March 1876, two months after the GWR had taken over working the lines west of Bristol.

Facing page: The premier train on the broad gauge was the 'Flying Dutchman', whose name — at first unofficial — was that of a well-known racehorse! The down train left Paddington daily at 11.45am and was allowed only 57min for the 53¼ miles to Didcot (two minutes more than the celebrated 'Exeter Express' in 1847, then the fastest train in the world), the 194 miles to Exeter being covered in 4½ hours. The up train, which left Exeter at 10.30am, was due at Paddington at 3.00pm. Both trains ran beyond Exeter, the down train arriving at Plymouth at 6.00pm and at Penzance at 9.00pm; though the up train commenced from Plymouth at 8.30am. From 1871 to 1884 these were the fastest trains in the world. The 'Flying Dutchman' is seen here between Maidenhead and Twyford on Jubilee Day in 1887, hauled by an 8ft 'Single'.

Above: West of Exeter the main line remained broad gauge until May 1892. In this view, an 8ft 'Single' heads an express train near Exeter, circa 1885. The original Brunel disc-and-crossbar signals were replaced by semaphores from 1877 onwards, the GWR having begun the replacement on its own lines in 1869. The signal on the right is of the old 'slotted' type, the signal being lowered through a slot in the post.

Above: A broad gauge express, around 1890, on which the brake vans are constructed using narrow gauge bodies mounted on broad gauge frames. The five clerestory carriages have wide bodies whilst the last carriage, to the rear of the brake van, is probably a composite slip carriage. Broad gauge bodies had generally ceased to be built after 1884, the later carriages having narrow bodies and frames running on broad-gauge bogies: it was possible to replace the bogies and change the gauge in about half-an-hour!

Above: The twilight of the broad gauge. The leading locomotive No. 3028, a 7ft 8in Dean 'Single', was one of eight such engines constructed to run on the broad gauge in August 1891, being designed to be easily convertible to the 'narrow gauge' by placing the wheels inside the double frames. Between 1876 and 1891, 121 'convertibles' ran on broad gauge metals, and the last converted locomotive was not withdrawn until May 1939! The photograph was taken at Paddington and the second locomotive is a Gooch 4—2—2 of the 'Rover' class (built between 1871 and 1888) and scrapped following the abolition of the broad gauge in May 1892.

Above: The Royal Albert Bridge, Saltash, under construction in 1859. The western (Saltash) span is already in position, while the eastern span is being raised and the masonry piers constructed beneath it. The approach viaduct on the Cornish side is complete, and that on the Devonshire side (right) is being built out towards the eastern pier. The eastern span was raised to its correct position by mid-December 1858, and on February 23 1859, Brunel reported that the superstructure was completed, also that the flooring had been completed and the ballast laid "and in two or three days the Bridge will be tested by the running of heavy trains across it". The bridge, which took four years to build, was opened to traffic on Monday May 2 1859. *Courtesy Science Museum.*

Right: A broadly similar viewpoint of the bridge on April 22 1880, by which time semaphore signalling had been installed. The very impressive appearance of the viaduct and the broad gauge baulk road are very clearly conveyed in this picture, and it is a measure of Brunel's achievement that the Royal Albert Bridge was opened less than 30 years after Stephenson's *Rocket* had triumphed at the Rainhill trials of 1830. More than 125 years after it opened.

CROSSING THE TAMAR

The Royal Albert Bridge, Saltash

THE carrying of the broad gauge baulk road across the River Tamar and into Cornwall presented both the Cornwall Railway and Brunel, as its Engineer, with a major challenge. The inherent difficulties to be faced in crossing such an expanse of water, 1,100ft wide and 70ft deep in the middle, were greatly increased when the Admiralty insisted that any bridge must have a clear headway of 100ft above the high water level, to allow sufficient clearance for the masts of the ships of the day. Brunel's original plan was to construct a bridge of one span of 255ft and six others of 105ft apiece, carried on timber-trussed arches, 80ft above high water. To comply with the requirements of the Admiralty, the design was twice altered, and eventually resulted in a design having only one central pier and two spans of 455ft each, to the piers on the two shores.

The foundation of the first pier, on the Saltash bank of the river, was laid on July 4 1853. The central pier was to be built with the aid of a giant iron cylinder, 37ft in diameter and 85ft high, and weighing 200 tons, which was used as a coffer dam. This was sunk in position in June 1854 and the water pumped out, so that work could begin on the construction of the pier foundations. All work was suspended for a time in October 1855 following the financial failure of the contractor, but the pier was finished by the late autumn of 1856.

The two great trusses for the main spans were built and completed on the Devonshire shore. A combination of the arched truss and suspension chain, with 11 upright standards connecting the two, they were 455ft long, 56ft high, and weighed 1,000 tons each. The western span was floated out on pontoons on September 1 1857, then raised three feet at a time by hydraulic presses under each end, the piers being constructed beneath as the span was gradually raised into position. This stage of the work was completed on May 19 1858, and the eastern truss was then floated into position on July 10 and was raised to its full height by mid-December.

Brunel had little to do with the work after the floating of the first span, as he was initially engaged with the launching of the *SS Great Eastern* and afterwards abroad due to the breakdown of his health, leading to his death in 1859. His Chief Assistant, R.P. Brereton, was left in sole charge, to complete the project.

Above: The full measure of Brunel's most impressive work can be seen in this view from the Devonshire bank of the Tamar. The bridge towered 100ft above the high water level — the need for this clearance being illustrated here by the masts of the sailing ship. The two main shore piers are entirely of masonry, as are all the approach piers carrying the side spans, while the central pier is of masonry to a height of 12ft, above high-water level, surmounted by four octagonal cast-iron columns, constructed in sections and connected by cast-iron openwork.

Right: From its opening (in 1859) the Cornwall Railway had been worked by the South Devon Railway, whose locomotive stock consisted entirely of saddle tanks, the majority of which were of either 4—4—0 or 0—6—0 types. There was little change in locomotive power after the GWR took over the working of the lines west of Bristol in 1876, as four-coupled saddle tanks were still working the service between Plymouth and Penzance on the last day of the broad gauge 16 years later. The apparent date of this photograph (April 22 1875) cannot be correct in view of the presence of bogie clerestory carriages in the up train about to pass onto the bridge, nor would the signals have been of the semaphore pattern until the 1880s. The photograph was probably taken circa 1890.

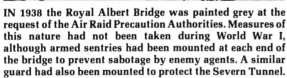

IN 1938 the Royal Albert Bridge was painted grey at the request of the Air Raid Precaution Authorities. Measures of this nature had not been taken during World War I, although armed sentries had been mounted at each end of the bridge to prevent sabotage by enemy agents. A similar guard had also been mounted to protect the Severn Tunnel.

Right: The painters — who appear to be working with a minimum of safety lines — at work on top of one of the 455ft spans, whose tubes were nearly 17ft in diameter. The central railings were added subsequent to construction, for they do not appear on any of the earlier photographs.

Above: A detailed view of one of the painters at work, more than 100ft above the Tamar. He is wearing no safety lines and the cradle itself is hung on a large hook beneath the pulley block only by means of a knot. The paint pot must have required frequent refilling!

Left: An interesting view from the bridge deck, which highlights the limited clearance for the single track, the climbing approach to the central pier, and the construction of the strengthening beams. The main arched wrought-iron upper tubes are strengthened by linked plates curved in the opposite direction to form ellipses which are 56ft deep at their centres. The single-track bridge deck is suspended from the two 455ft spans by 11 pairs of symmetrically-spaced vertical members, linked by cross-braces and diagonal trusses, as shown here. The outward thrust of the arched tubes was therefore countered by the inward pull of the suspension linkage.

Right: On June 18 1938, the up 'Cornish Riviera' express headed by No.5011 *Tintagel Castle,* passes beneath the workmen engaged on the painting operation. No.5011 spent more than 25 years working from Newton Abbot shed, to which it was sent when new in July 1927, though its last years until withdrawal in September 1962 were spent at Old Oak Common, London.

NARROW GAUGE SCENES
OF THE
NINETEENTH CENTURY

Above: A unique photograph of considerable historic importance: 'narrow gauge' 0—6—0 No. 35, reconstructed at Wolverhampton in February 1866 (together with the similar No. 34) from an ex-Shrewsbury & Chester Railway 0—4—0, with an intermediate crankshaft. No. 35 always worked in the far north of the GWR system, in the Chester area. The locomotive is pictured at Wolverhampton, circa 1875, undergoing a heavy repair in the open air, owing to the limited space available at Stafford Road Works. What appears to be a group of engineering pupils are assisting a regular gang of fitters, under a chargehand. This is thought to be the only known photograph of one of these engines, previously thought never to have been photographed. No. 35 was withdrawn in October 1889, having recorded 262,221 miles in service. A selection of fireirons are leaning against the accommodation bogie under the smokebox, whilst the gang are working on pistons (left) and axleboxes (on the wooden trestles). Note the number 35 painted on the cab panel.

COMMENCING life as the promoter of a broad gauge railway from London to Bristol, the GWR soon became part of a broad gauge empire (much of which it did not own) which eventually extends southwards to Weymouth and westwards to Penzance. It had also reached New Milford in West Wales, Hereford (via Gloucester) in Welsh Marches, and as far north as Wolverhampton, where it came to the end of its expansion, having met what was ultimately to be its supplanter — the 'narrow gauge'. Not that the latter was anyting new, as the GWR had previously been engaged in a bitter conflict with the 4ft 8½in gauge, represented primarily by the London & South Western Railway.

The significant development was that the only way for the GWR to expand any further north was over the lines of existing companies, all of which were of the lesser gauge. North of Wolverhampton, there was already a 'narrow gauge' route to Shrewsbury, Chester and Birkenhead, owned by

three small companies, the Shrewsbury & Birmingham, the Shrewsbury & Chester, and the Birkenhead Railways. The two Shrewsbury companies worked in close harmony, not least in defending themselves against the machinations of the LNWR, and they were soon working in equal harmony with the GWR which was their only ally. The acquiring of the smaller railways by amalgamation, followed by the laying of a third rail to extend the broad gauge at least to Chester, if not to Birkenhead, appeared to be the logical outcome of this alliance.

Alas, for the GWR's hopes, although the required Bill was passed, the amalgamation being described as "being of a special character and of great importance to the public interest" (the former probably being the amalgamation of two different gauges!) one of the provisions was that the extension northwards of the broad gauge was forbidden. Thus, when in 1854 the GWR amalgamated with the SBR, the only possible action

Above: 2—2—2 No. 378 *Sir Daniel* the first 'narrow gauge' express passenger engine to be built at Swindon, in September 1866. Designed by Joseph Armstrong who had moved to Swindon from Wolverhampton when Daniel Gooch resigned in October 1864, the 30 engines of this class worked between London and Wolverhampton, via both Birmingham and Worcester, and also on the South Wales trains, after conversion to 'narrow gauge', in 1872. No. 378 is pictured in the lower yard at Stafford Road shed, circa 1878, shortly after the fitting of number plates — prior to 1876, GWR 'narrow gauge' engines had painted numbers. This was one of three engines which were always in the Northern Division, and No. 378 was at one time shedded at Birkenhead to work the up and down 'Zulu' trains — the 11.45am Birkenhead-Paddington and 4.45pm Paddington-Birkenhead services to and from Wolverhampton. Note that there are no brakes on the engine, only on the tender, and that the front buffers are unsprung! No. 378 was withdrawn in May 1898, though the majority of the class were reconstructed as 0—6—0 goods engines between 1900 and 1902, two of which survived until 1919 and 1920 respectively.

Above: The majority of the goods engines acquired by the GWR from various absorbed lines were soon replaced by engines of Armstrong's 'Standard Goods' class, of which more than 300 were built between 1866 and 1876. They had the same size cylinders (17in x 24in), and boilers as the express passenger engines of the 'Sir Daniel' class, and like the latter engines originally had only weatherboards to protect the crew and painted numbers on the cabsides. No. 1188 was one of the last of the class to be built (in 1876) and is seen here circa 1880. The locomotive was withdrawn in November 1927, its final years having been spent at St. Philip's Marsh shed, Bristol. The Armstrong 'Standard Goods' engines were used on a wide variety of duties throughout the GWR system — including the broad gauge, as 20 examples (Nos. 1196-1215) were converted between 1884 and 1888 to run on Brunel's 'baulk road' for the haulage of through goods trains between London and Plymouth. They often worked passenger trains including, on occasion, main line and cross-country express duties, the latter work continuing as late as 1920. The broad gauge examples were reconverted to 4ft 8½in gauge post-1892. During the First World War, 22 examples were sold to the British government for service in Serbia and Salonika: four of these engines remained in service in Turkey until the 1930s, when the last handful of GWR examples were also withdrawn after 60 years hard work. Originally fitted with 140psi boilers, the class was subsequently rebuilt with 180psi boilers of around a dozen different types. Also, although the class were originally fitted with 5ft diameter driving wheels, the subsequent fitting of thicker tyres increased the diameter to 5ft 2in.

was to extend the 'narrow gauge' southwards! Pressure for this course of action was increased by the Oxford Worcester & Wolverhampton Railway (justly known as the 'Old Worse and Worse') which was supposed to be a broad gauge line, but which had only 'narrow gauge' engines and rolling stock — though it did have the third rail throughout its main line! By 1861, the third rail reached London and brought the 4ft 8½in gauge to Paddington; thankfully, Brunel did not live to see that dreadful day.

The legacy of the 1854 amalgamation, which was followed in 1863 by amalgamation with the West Midland Railway (as the OWWR had become), meant that the GWR had lines, locomotives, carriages and wagons on two gauges; and that there were two locomotive works, at Swindon and Wolverhampton, responsible for two Divisions under two Superintendents — though Swindon was in overall control. This situation continued for more than 40 years, as the end of the broad gauge in 1892 did not immediately end the Northern Division's distinctive locomotive practice.

Left: The Newport Abergavenny & Hereford Railway was another 'narrow gauge' line eventually acquired by the GWR (as part of the West Midland Railway), and the Crumlin Viaduct, on its branch to Quaker's Yard, was the longest and highest structure of its kind in Great Britain, when it was opened in May 1857. It was 1,650ft long, in two sections divided by the summit of an intervening hill, the main eastern section being 1,066ft in length and 200ft high. Construction began in 1854, and this is thought to be the only known photograph of the construction of one of the cast-iron piers during the initial stages of the work. It later formed part of the through route between Pontypool Road and Neath, which was closed in June 1964. Crumlin Viaduct had been scheduled for preservation, but receiving no maintenance after closure, its ageing fabric deteriorated rapidly, and it was demolished in 1967.

The viaduct had been designed by T.W. Kennard and although originally double track, the metals over the viaduct were subsequently singled, train control being provided by electric staff between signal boxes on either side. The maximum rail height above the River Ebbw was 220ft, and GWR locomotives which worked across the viaduct included 2—8—0s of both '2800' and ROD types, together with 0—6—0 and 2—6—2 tank engines and 2—6—0 and 0—6—0 tender classes. Prior to the transfer of LMS traffic to the Merthyr-Abergavenny route, coal from collieries around Treharris to Birkenhead and the north had been worked over Crumlin viaduct by LNWR 0—6—0 saddletanks.

Right: The excavation of the Severn Tunnel, powers for which were obtained by the GWR in 1872, was the greatest and most expensive engineering project ever undertaken by a railway company. Work commenced on the Monmouthshire side of the Severn on March 18 1873, but the last length of brickwork in the tunnel was not finished until April 18 1885! For more than a year during 1879-80, all work had to be abandoned due to the inrush of the Great Spring, until heroic action by a diver named Lambert enabled a flood door in a heading 340 yards under the river to be closed. The tunnel was 7,666 yards long, nearly 76½ million bricks were used in its construction and the greatest number of men working on the tunnel at one time was 3,628. The total cost of the tunnel and new lines on either side of the entrances was £1,806,248. A special train, with Sir Daniel and Lady Gooch and a party of friends, was able to make the first journey from Severn Tunnel Junction through the tunnel into the cutting on the Gloucestershire side and back, on September 5 1885. A few months later, on January 9 1886, an experimental coal train of 14 wagons and two vans, which left Aberdare at 9.50am for Southampton, passed through the tunnel, resulting, as the Directors proudly reported during February: "in coal which had been raised at the Colliery in the morning being delivered at the Port in the evening of the same day". However, the new line was not opened for regular goods traffic until September 1 due to the need to install a large Guibal fan, 40ft in diameter and 12ft wide, to ventilate the tunnel, and passenger trains did not commence running between Bristol and Cardiff until December 1 1886. This view shows excavations for the approach cutting to the tunnel on the Monmouthshire side of the Severn, near Portskewett, circa 1875.

The greatest difficulty encountered in the construction of the Severn Tunnel was the constant inrush of water, and all parts of the excavation had to be shored with timber. In some parts, penetration by water was so bad that the timbering had to be completely roofed with felt or corrugated iron to enable the bricklayers to work successfully. One commentator said: "In other places the water poured in in such quantities under great pressure and spurting upwards and downwards in all directions that it was impossible to keep any lights burning, and, until the installation of the electric light the work had to be done almost on the dark."

Right, upper: Prior to the opening of the Severn Tunnel, passengers travelling between Cardiff and Bristol had either to travel via Gloucester (and the Midland Railway) or cross the Severn by means of a ferry which plied between Portskewett Pier and New Passage, near Pilning. The ferry, together with the piers and short connecting branches opened in 1864. Portskewett station is seen here prior to 1886, showing the branch to the pier, on the right, behind the down platform. The branch and the pier were both closed and dismantled immediately after the tunnel came into use. The South Wales Railway had originally been broad gauge, but was 'narrowed' in 1872, hence the extra width between the running lines. Note the unusual loading gauge over the siding on the left.

Right, lower: A few miles away, on the line which followed the River Wye from Chepstow to Monmouth, Tintern station served a notable beauty spot famous since the time of William Wordsworth's poem, 'On the Wye above Tintern'. Opened November 1 1876, the Wye Valley Railway was always worked by the GWR, but was not absorbed until July 1905. In this view of Tintern, an early saloon carriage stands on the loop line behind the down platform, in front of the signal box. The date is circa 1900. Alas, passengers no longer wait for trains at Tintern, as the line was closed to passenger trains on January 5 1959 and to all traffic from January 6 1964. However, both the station and signalbox have been faithfully rebuilt as the centre-pieces of a picnic site and exhibition area.

Left: Lineside apparatus allowing the railway's Travelling Post Office vehicles to collect mail without stopping was first introduced at Yatton, on the BER, in 1859. In 1866, Post Office huts and gear were installed on the Cornwall Railway at St. Germans, Menheniot, Doublebois, Bodmin Road, Burngullow and Grampound Road; but in 1871 Bodmin Road's equipment was transferred to Lostwithiel, the Bodmin residents having requested that the Night Mail should call at Bodmin Road. The up 'Mail' from Penzance is seen here, with clerestory TPO No.839 (built in 1894), collecting mail at Menheniot, watched by a Post Office official, circa 1900.

Right: A picture rich in GWR 'atmosphere' —
Yeovil (Pen Mill) Station in the early 1900s,
showing the overall roof which was once a
common feature of GWR stations. The line to
Yeovil was opened as a single broad gauge line
on September 1 1856, and was extended to
Dorchester and Weymouth a few months later.
The Weymouth line was doubled in 1858, and
converted to the 'narrow gauge' in June 1874 —
though the Bristol & Exeter branch from
Durston to Yeovil remained broad gauge for a
further five years. Passenger services between
Yeovil (Pen Mill) and Yeovil Junction were
withdrawn on May 6 1968.

Above and right: 2—4—0 No.213 was a
locomotive with a history of more than usual
interest. It was built by Beyer Peacock in 1861
as one of six 2—2—2s for the West Midland
Railway (WMR No. 104), but was rebuilt as a
2—4—0 at Wolverhampton in October 1883 —
as were its companions and six very similar
engines which had always been 2—4—0s, to
form the '196' class. In December 1911 it was
sold, together with No.212, to Mr. A.R. Angus
who used the pair to demonstrate his system of
automatic train control, as illustrated here, on
a section of the West Somerset Mineral
Railway at Watchet. They then passed to the
Bute Works Supply Co. who sold them in March
1921 to the Cambrian Railways, where they
became CR Nos.1(212) and 10(213). The
following year the railway Grouping brought
them back into GWR stock as Nos.1329 and
1328 respectively. No.1328 was withdrawn in
August 1926 and No.1329 in November 1927.

Not quite the 19th Century, but certainly narrow gauge! The Vale of Rheidol Light Railway was opened from Aberystwyth to Devil's Bridge in 1902, and became part of the Cambrian Railways system in July 1913. Pictured here at Devil's Bridge is 2—6—2T No. 1 *Edward VII,* one of two identical engines built by Davies & Metcalfe (a firm usually associated with the manufacture of injectors) in 1902, the second engine being named *Prince of Wales.* However, Becoming GWR No. 1212 in 1922, *Edward VII* was withdrawn in December 1932. However, its twin (GWR No. 1213) was rebuilt by the GWR during 1923, when its Stephenson link motion was replaced by Walschaerts valve gear, and is still in service as No. 9 *Prince of Wales,* having regained the name it lost during Cambrian ownership. Also still at work today are the two similar engines built at Swindon in 1923, Nos. 7 *Owain Glyndwr* and 8 *Llywelyn.* These are the only steam locomotives in British Rail's stock.

THE GWR was often styled the 'Royal Road', owing to the regular use of its services by members of the royal family travelling between London and Windsor. At the Centenary Banquet of the GWR on October 30 1935, HRH the Prince of Wales (later HRH King Edward VIII, and subsequently HRH the Duke of Windsor) recalled how from its earliest days the GWR had been a link between the Sovereign and the Government, referring to the constant visits to Windsor of Prime Ministers, members of the Cabinet and other distinguished persons travelling during the days of Queen Victoria. He continued: "Indeed, your company, your great company, deserves its name of the 'Royal Road' if only for the fact that it was on your wheels that Queen Victoria first experienced railroad travel, and because it was on your lines that she was borne on her last journey home". The royal family travelled further afield of course, and this chapter provides a flavour of the GWR's well-organised royal train operations.

THE

ROYAL ROAD

Facing page: The royal funeral train for HRH Queen Victoria left from Paddington's No.8 platform, on the arrival side of Paddington Station on February 2 1901, hauled by 4—4—0 No.3373 which was specially named *Royal Sovereign* **for the occasion, in place of its original name** *Atbara.* **The name** *Royal Sovereign* **was normally carried by Dean 6ft 8in 'Single' No.3050. The 40 'Atbaras' built in 1900-1 were the first locomotives to be built with the features which became a hall-mark of Churchward's standard boilers: a Belpaire firebox and a domeless boiler barrel — though as yet the latter was parallel and not tapered. The straight tops to the frames and the severe, cast-iron chimney were other new features. As No.4120,** *Atbara* **was withdrawn in September 1930. The three white discs in place of the usual headlamps appears to have been a unique instance of such usage on the GWR. Note also the communication cord, threaded through the 'eyes' mounted above the tender coal-rails.**

Above: An interesting view of the ornately opulent funeral carriage used for Queen Victoria's funeral, in February 1901. In the mirror at the far end of the carriage can be seen reflected the image of the tripod and camera used to take the photograph.

Above, left: In 1907 a royal visit to Cardiff took place when HRH King Edward VII, accompanied by HRH Queen Alexandra, opened the new docks. The special train inside the dock area was hauled by the Cardiff Railway 0—4—0ST No. 6, built by Kitsons of Leeds in 1899. Later GWR No. 1339, it was scrapped in June 1934, though its identical twin, No. 1338 (formerly CR No. 5) is preserved at Bleadon & Uphill station.

Above, right: Another view of CR No.6, looking more like a carnival float than a locomotive! Note the shape of the buffers, designed to prevent buffer-locking on sharp curves. This was the only occasion on which a royal train ran over the Cardiff Railway, whose system was largely confined within the area of Cardiff Docks. This was also the first occasion on which any of the South Wales railways had such a royal privilege — the only other occasion being in 1912 when the Taff Vale Railway provided a royal train for HRH King George V. On this occasion, the GWR provided the stock, for at that time the CR had no carriages of its own.

Above: Another royal docks tour was the occasion of this scene at Avonmouth on July 9 1908. The GWR royal train, pictured here, was provided in 1897, as part of a present to Queen Victoria on the occasion of her Diamond Jubilee, and was chiefly used to carry the Queen and her Suite from Paddington to Windsor. By the Queen's express command, the old private apartments in the royal carriage itself (the third vehicle) had to remain unchanged — hence the peculiar shape of the roof with it's domed central section. The remaining five vehicles' roof profile had obvious affinities with the American Pullman car of that time. Known as the 'Royal' clerestory, only five other carriages were built with similar roofs, among them being Churchward's celebrated dynamometer car, No.730. This royal train is said to have cost the GWR in excess of £40,000. How much the special station, built for this occasion, cost the Dock Authorities is not known! The domeless 0—6—0ST, No.2131 is one of the '2101' class (a domeless variation of the '2021' class) built at Wolverhampton between 1902 and 1905, which marked the spread of Churchward's influence to the Northern Division Works. The 140 engines of the '2021' and '2101' classes were in great demand for dock areas and colliery lines, but did not usually reach such prestigious heights as hauling the royal train: one imagines that this was a unique occasion. Built in August 1903, No.2131 was rebuilt with pannier tanks in August 1924, when it also received a domed boiler, and was not withdrawn until November 1951. After working at Bristol for many years, it was then shedded at Hereford and spent its last years in the Forest of Dean, at Lydney — where at least it worked in a royal forest!

Left: The funeral of HRH King Edward VII on May 20 1910 was another important occasion for the GWR, as the late King was to be buried at Windsor. This special 'Farewell' tribute was placed over the entrance to the arrival side at Paddington: note the absence of the familiar arched roof of later years, as the extra arrival platforms were not added until 1913. Just visible inside the station are the inclined rows of seats provided especially for the dignitaries attending the royal funeral. Curiously, several black umbrellas are in evidence, despite bright, sunny weather. These were probably for protection from the sun, as the solemnity of the occasion probably ruled out the use of parasols.

Below: At this time, the GWR had no recognised royal engine, but No.4021 *King Edward*, one of Churchward's 'Star' class, was the obvious choice for this occasion. No.4021 is pictured standing at platform 8 in Paddington station, waiting for the arrival of the funeral cortege.

Right: The Royal funeral train at Windsor station, where the GWR had provided a special royal waiting room and a great glazed roof for Queen Victoria's Diamond Jubilee in 1897, as well as the new royal train. The royal waiting room is the building on the left, and the coffin has just been placed on a gun carriage to be hauled by a team of sailors to St. George's Chapel.

Left: "The Captains and the Kings depart" (Kipling); and the driver of No.4021 turns his back on pomp and ceremony to oil the outside motion of his engine before returning to Old Oak Common from Windsor. Note the brakes fitted to the bogie wheels — a Churchward feature which was not subsequently perpetuated as standard GWR locomotive practice.

Right, above: The driver and fireman of the Royal funeral train, pictured on the footplate of No.4021 at Windsor station. The letters 'PN' on the cabside just below the roof are thought to be a previously unrecorded example of an early GWR shed code, for whilst Old Oak Common shed was always known as Paddington, the code in later years was 'PDN'. The earlier practice was for a metal strip or stencilled letters to be carried inside the cab, but this did not become the norm until several years after this photograph was taken.

Right, below: The immaculately-dressed Windsor Station Master inspects the Royal Coat of Arms carried by No.4021. It was only to be expected that Windsor would be one of the GWR stations whose station master was of the 'top hat' elite. Even though this was a special occasion and the GWR would have been particularly determined to provide a faultless, immaculately clean service, photographs like this powerfully project the pre-Grouping splendour of Britain's railways.

Left: The new monarch. Collett 'King' class No.6029 (formerly *King Stephen*) was renamed *King Edward VIII* in May 1936, and is seen here speeding through Old Oak Common on May 22 1936, on its first run after being renamed. Built at Swindon in 1930, No.6029 served the GWR and BR for 35 years before being withdrawn in July 1962. The 4—6—0 was scrapped at Cashmore's Newport yard in November 1962. Four 'Kings' were dismantled at this location, the others being: Nos.6009 *King Charles II*, 6019 *King Henry V*, and 6021 *King Richard II*.

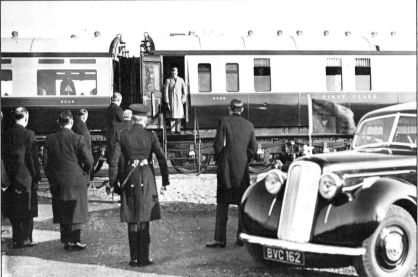

Right: HRH King Edward VIII leaving the royal train at Llantwit Major, South Wales, to enter his Humber car, in November 1936. No.9005 (left) was one of two first class brake saloons, incorporating a dining saloon and kitchen, built in 1930, while No.9068 (right) was a first class sleeping car built in 1931. Edward VIII's reign was short and unhappy: he succeeded to the throne on January 20 1936 following the death of his father George V, at Sandringham, at the age of 70, but abdicated the crown on December 11 1936, — shortly after this picture was taken — because of the constitutional crisis precipitated by his relationship with Wallis Simpson, an American divorcee who he later married. Edward VIII's younger brother, the Duke of York, thus became King George VI in 1937.

Left: The special royal train headlights: note that the extra-large lamps and the crowns were separate items. No.4082 *Windsor Castle* became the regular royal engine after it was driven by HRH King George V on the occasion of the royal visit to Swindon Works in 1924.

THE
HOLIDAY LINE

ANOTHER title claimed by the GWR was that of 'the Holiday Line', a description which often appeared in its advertisements and publications. Although serving other holiday areas, such as West Wales and North Wales, it was the West Country which was always regarded as being the most important and which came to be synonymous with the Company's holiday traffic.

From the time of its introduction in July 1904, the 'Cornish Riviera Express' was always the GWR's premier train; it was also one of the most famous trains in Great Britain, and became one of only four 'titled trains' to retain its name throughout the Second World War, the others being the LNER's 'Flying Scotsman', 'Aberdonian' and 'Night Scotsman' services.

Non-stop running between Paddington and Plymouth (245 miles via Bristol) first took place on March 10, 1902, by no less a person than His Royal Highness King Edward VII, on the occasion of his return from the

opening of the Royal Naval College at Dartmouth. This created a new world record — the previous one being the GWR's Paddington to Exeter non-stop run, in the down direction, by another Royal special in July 1903 — and was followed by the announcement that there was to be a new Paddington to Penzance express which would not stop between London and Plymouth!

The new train was to be limited to seven carriages, and the main portion, including a dining car, was to run to and from Penzance, while there was also to be a Falmouth 'through carriage'. As part of the publicity for

the new train, a public competition was held to suggest the most suitable name for the service. Amongst the names suggested were 'Cornish Riviera Limited' and 'Royal Duchy Express' — the latter anticipating a British Railways' introduction more than 50 years later. James Inglis, the GWR's General Manager, selected 'Riviera Express', to which the word 'Cornish' was soon added — and whilst the train was officially being shown in the time tables as the 'Cornish Riviera Limited Express', this was soon shortened by the staff to 'The Limited'.

From July 1906, the new train was

Above: The 'Cornish Riviera Express' at No.1 platform in 1912. Formed of the latest Churchward 'Toplight' stock, with three clerestory carriages at the rear included in the slip portions, the train is painted in the crimson lake livery which had been recently introduced by the GWR. The station clock on the right indicates that, despite still loading, the train's booked departure time (10.30am) is approaching, when it should move smartly away on it's non-stop run to Plymouth — though a service stop for an assistant engine was often required at Newton Abbot.

transferred to the long-awaited, shorter route to the West of England, via Westbury, and departure time was changed from 10.10am to what became the legendary 10.30am: hence the title of one of the GWR's splendid publications 'for boys of all ages', 'The 10-30 Limited'. From Paddington the 'Limited' had no less than three slip portions attached to the rear, for Weymouth (slipped at Westbury), for Minehead and Ilfracombe (slipped at Taunton) and a final slip portion at Exeter, initially for the Torquay line but later altered to run forward to Kingsbridge. The main train now had carriages for Falmouth. St. Ives and Penzance, and on summer Saturdays the 'Limited' often ran in three, or even four parts. On one celebrated occasion in 1926 (see page 42) the train ran in five portions! The up train was never so famous: it left Penzance at 10.00am and was due at Paddington at 4.45pm.

Above: This evocative photograph was taken in June 1923, when the 'Star' 4—6—0s (introduced 1907) were still the GWR's premier express engines, always to be found at the head of the prestigious 'Cornish Riviera Express'. Despite the arrival of Collett's 'Castles' two months later, it was not until 1925 that 'The Limited' ceased to be a regular 'Star' class working. In this view, No.4049 *Princess Maud* is still in the overall green livery, without lining, introduced during the war years, and with the copper cap of the chimney and the brass safety valve 'bonnet' painted over. The driver is adding some last-minute oil to the small end of the connecting rod, while the young boy adjacent to the cab apparently dreams of taking over his job. *Princess Maud's* crew will be more-than-usually on their toes on the forthcoming journey — for the bowler-hatted silhouette visible in the cab spectacle window indicates that a Footplate Inspector is on board! Built in May 1914, No.4049 was withdrawn from service in July 1953, from Stafford Road shed, Wolverhampton, having run more than two million miles for the GWR and BR. The 'Stars' of George Jackson Churchward were the foremost passenger locomotives of the first two decades of the 20th Century — no other engines in Britain could run as fast, or as hard, with express passenger trains. A total of 72 were built between 1907 and 1922 and they were popular and successful in traffic. Many fine runs were recorded, but one outstanding performance in 1925 is worth recalling, when No.4026 *King Richard* hauled a 550-ton up West of England express from Taunton to Paddington (143 miles) in 152 minutes! 'Stars' names also included 'Knights', 'Kings', 'Queens', 'Princes', 'Princesses' and 'Abbeys' and the final survivor was No. 4056 *Princess Margaret*, withdrawn in October 1957.

Right: The GWR's Publicity Department was astute and forceful in its promotion of the Company's routes and services for holiday purposes. In this delightful Edwardian scene, a gentleman and lady examine an extensive promotional map and display, possibly to plan a holiday on the English 'Riviera Coast'. Note that litter is not a new phenomenon!

Above: Following the General Strike in May 1926, the GWR did not introduce its Summer time table, but restored the ordinary service, to which it added numerous additional trains at the weekends, as required. On one notable Saturday in July, the 'Cornish Riviera Express' was run in no fewer than five portions, the five engines being 'backed down' to the station, from Old Oak Common, coupled together. The GWR made sure that this event received the maximum possible publicity by inviting the press along to witness this unique occurrence! The leading engine is 'Star' class No.4056 *Princess* *Margaret*, the last of the class to remain in service, until withdrawal in October 1957, from Bristol Bath Road Shed. Second in line is 'Saint' class No.2907 *Lady Disdain* which — in the contrast to No.4056 — was an early withdrawal, in July 1933 (from Newport). The other engines are two 'Stars' and a 'Castle', which is probably No.4093 *Dunster Castle* (of Old Oak Common). The 4—6—0 is coupled to one of the new high-sided 4,000 gallon tenders and No.4093 was probably the first engine to be so equipped. The 'Star' behind No.2907 is paired with one of the ten 'intermediate' 3,500 gallon tenders built during 1925.

Right: Inside Paddington station on the same Saturday in July 1926, and the reason for the line-up of the five express engines is apparent. Crowds of holiday-makers throng the departure platforms, and the assorted luggage items include 'personal transport' in the shape of cycles and prams. Note the barrow full of carriage tail lamps in the foreground on No.4 platform.

Left, above: The Jubilee of the 'Cornish Riviera Express', July 8 1929, with the train of new extra-wide carriage stock awaiting departure for the West behind Collett 'King' 4—6—0 No. 6000 *King George V.* Built specifically for the 'Limited', the new 9ft 7in wide carriages were electrically lit, and electric fans and extractors were fitted in the dining saloons and kitchen cars. Galvanised steel panelling was used for the outside panelling and roof, whilst Empire-grown timber used for internal fitting-out included teak, gurjin, Borneo white mahogany and Honduras mahogany. The new stock was fireproofed and the steel underframes were carried on 9ft bolster-type bogies. The 13-carriage formation carried 428 passengers in compartments and 119 in the restaurant cars; total weight was 448 tons 16cwt. By 1929 the GWR claimed that in its 25 years of service the 'Limited' had run more than 5 million miles, and carried more than 3 million passengers.

Left, below: A glorious image of a very proud age indeed. The footplate crews and guards who worked 'The Limited' often received considerable publicity, not least on the occasion of their retirement from the Company's service. Pictured here on May 22 1926 is GWR Guard Tom Willie (right) who was retiring after 50 years service with 'the Company', as the GWR was always known to its intensely loyal staff. The original Topical Press caption records that one of Mr. Willie's duties had been to Guard Princess Mary's honeymoon train. The other gentlemen present are (left-right): P.N. Mansfield MBS (Station Master at Paddington); H.R. Campfield (Divisional Superintendent) and Tom Gooding (Head Guard of the 'Cornish Riviera Express'). This picture illustrates that 'the Limited' did not always depart from Paddington's famous platform No. 1 — the train is shown here at platform No. 3.

Below: The GWR also tried to attract press attention when its senior footplatemen retired, and on this occasion Driver Lakey was stepping down from the cab for the last time after 49 years service, latterly as a regular driver of the 'Cornish Riviera Express'. He is pictured here standing on the running plate of his spotless 'King' class 4—6—0, at the conclusion of his final run, on October 18 1930. He is being congratulated by J.W. Kislingbury, H.R. Campfield (Divisional Superintendent) and P.N. Mansfield (Paddington Station Master).

Right: Holidaymakers from a more leisured class, and in a more leisurely age, arriving at Henley-on-Thames for the Regatta on July 5 1911. Henley-on-Thames was the terminus of a branch line from Twyford, opened in June 1857. The line was doubled in 1898, and in 1910 the platform canopy was extended by 200ft to cater for occasions such as this, while a 55ft turntable allowed special trains to be worked from Paddington by large tender engines. Henley always received favoured treatment, there being numerous first class season ticket holders. In 1902 there were three through trains daily to Paddington and five from Paddington, one of which was a slip carriage off the 9.15pm 'South Wales Mail'. On Wednesdays and Saturdays, a further 'slip' off the 12.15am 'Birkenhead corridor train' enabled those spending an evening 'in town' to arrive back at Henley at 1.20am!

A quite delightful scene at Torquay station in 1922, prior to the down platform being extended beyond the signal box. A '4500' class 2—6—2T stands on the wagon turntable serving several short sidings originally used for off-loading the numerous horses and carriages which accompanied wealthy families visiting Torquay for 'the season' — then the winter months. The up platform had been lengthened when the line to Paignton was doubled in 1910, but the down platform remained hopelessly inadequate for the summer holiday traffic, which increased annually. Extension was authorised in March 1911. Another '4500' class 2—6—2T heads a down passenger train of bogie clerestory stock, the first vehicle being a slip carriage, as indicated by the vacuum reservoirs on the roof. Until the late 1920s, large tender engines were not allowed to work beyond Paignton to Kingswear, and the 2—6—2Ts were used for most trains.

Above: The increasing popularity of Weston-super-Mare as a holiday resort brought both increased revenues and increasing problems to the GWR on account of the number of extra trains to be accommodated. A separate 'excursion' station was opened at Locking Road in 1914, in addition to a special excursion platform, which had been provided some years earlier. Locking Road station, with four platform faces, was adjacent to the former BER broad gauge terminus, which had been replaced by a new station when the loop line (always 'narrow gauge') was opened in March 1884. In this view of Locking Road, circa 1924, an excursion train has arrived at platform 2 in the charge of No.3818 *County of Radnor,* one of Churchward's outside cylinder 4—4—0s known as 'Churchward's rough riders'. Built between 1904 and 1912, all 40 engines were withdrawn by 1934; No. 3818 was withdrawn in August 1931. Locking Road closed on September 7 1964.

Above: Not all of the GWR's holiday trains ran to and from London, nor did they all serve resorts on the Company's system. October 1922 saw the reintroduction of the Birkenhead and Folkstone through service (withdrawn during the war), seen here on the first day of the new service, at Guildford. The carriage destination board carries one of the longest descriptions ever employed: 'Birkenhead, Chester, Birmingham, Oxford, Reading, Folkestone, Dover and Deal'. A few years later, Ramsgate and Margate were added to the list, but only Birkenhead remained from the GWR stations. The carriage (No.7465) is a corridor composite built in 1902, with electric lighting.

Left: Another new GWR service, commencing in July 1922, was a restaurant car train operating between Cardiff and Brighton, and for the first few months, this involved a partnership with two other railways, the LSWR and the LBSCR. In this view, 'Saint' class 4—6—0 No. 2922 *St. Gabriel* enters Newport Station from Cardiff on the first day of the new service, with a train of very mixed stock. The train at the down platform, consisting of an 0—6—0ST with low-roofed four or six-wheeled carriages, is typical of the local trains serving the Monmouthshire Valleys. The engine adjacent to the signal box appears to be a '3600' class 2—4—2T, one of 31 engines built between 1900 and 1903 for the London and Birmingham suburban services, though one or two were always in South Wales. In 1922, No. 3612 was shedded at Newport. Note the enamel advertisements placed beneath the platform edge, urging GWR patrons to 'Furnish at Gane's: Newport, Cardiff, Bristol.'

Just over an hour later on the same day, No. 2922 and its train stand in Bath Spa Station before continuing to Westbury and Salisbury where the LSWR will take over. Opened in 1840, Bath Spa was one of Brunel's original stations, with an overall roof which was demolished in the 1890s when the platforms were lengthened. A notable feature of the station was the large signal box high above the down platform. No. 2922, built in September 1907, remained in service until December 1944, its last shed being Severn Tunnel Junction.

OVERSEAS CONNECTIONS
FISHGUARD

Above: A general view of Fishguard Harbour station in 1907. Both the harbour and station had been planned by the GWR's Engineer, James Inglis. In the foreground are cattle trucks for the Irish cattle traffic. An iron 'Mink' and two bolster wagons are to the rear of the cattle wagons, on the right, while a '633' class 0—6—0 side tank is shunting. The dozen engines of this class, built at Wolverhampton in 1871-2, were the first inside-framed engines of their type on the GWR, apart from two early engines built at Swindon in 1860. The track on the left ran back through quarry workings to Fishguard & Goodwick station, where the engine shed was also sited. Modellers should note the splendid bracketed signals!

ONE of Brunel's imaginative plans was to construct a main line to Fishguard, which he envisaged becoming the main port for cross-channel traffic to Southern Ireland. In the event, Neyland (which the GWR renamed New Milford) became the terminus of the South Wales Railway and the port for Ireland, owing to the effects of the economic depression of the period and the dreadful Irish Famine during the late 1840s.

However, in 1906 a new main line was opened from Clarbeston Road to Fishguard, where a magnificent new harbour and station had been constructed at great cost. Another new port had also been created at Rosslare, in Ireland, which replaced Waterford (previously the twin port with New Milford) and a new line was opened westwards to join the existing Waterford to Dublin, Limerick and Mallow (for Cork and Killarney) lines. The GWR shared with the Great Southern & Western Railway of Ireland both the cost and the ownership of these new works.

In addition to the normal cross-channel traffic, the GWR introduced some spectacular day excursions to Killarney, the first of which, on September 24 1907, was the occasion of the first (and only) non-stop run from Paddington to Fishguard, a distance of 261.4 miles. This was made by the 4-4-0 'City' class engine No. 3408 *Ophir* which was specially renamed *Killarney* for the occasion, and which retained that name until withdrawal in 1929.

However, the GWR had ambitions far beyond the regular traffic to and from the South of Ireland or the occasional day excursion, however spectacular it might be. The considerable experience in handling ocean traffic at Plymouth, from the German liners en route from New York to Hamburg, suggested that it might be possible to develop similar traffic at Fishguard in connection with British ships sailing to North America on the North Atlantic run, all of which then berthed at Liverpool. The LNWR had already invited the White Star Line to put passengers ashore at Holyhead to cut the passage time and avoid possible delay by fog in the Mersey. The GWR responded by setting its sights on the rival Cunard Line which it wanted to entice to use Fishguard. Not only was the journey from Fishguard to London slightly shorter than that from Holyhead, but ocean liners could put into harbour in South Wales five hours earlier than at

Left: Fishguard in April 1908, looking towards Fishguard & Goodwick. The GWR's Fishguard Bay Hotel (formerly the Wyncliff Hotel) is situated among the trees on the hillside. The numerous wagons include cattle trucks (which are 'limed' to stop the spread of disease) and a train of loaded coal wagons — probably for the bunkers of the cross-channel steamers. Note the shunting capstan between the two signal posts (lower right). Once again, lineside hardware to interest the railway modeller includes the signalling, the double armed loading gauge on the left, and the shunting capstan between the signals on the right

Holyhead. Thus, their cargoes and passengers could be in London by the time that the rival line's passengers were landing in North Wales.

There were even greater ambitions, for many passengers from the United States of America were usually bound for the continent, and the GWR was preparing to run through Ocean specials from Fishguard to Dover, in conjunction with the South Eastern & Chatham Railway. Roof boards were prepared in readiness, lettered 'Cunard Ocean Express: Fishguard to Dover'.

Cunard liners continued to call at Fishguard regularly from six to eight times a month until the outbreak of the war, three or four special trains

usually being run to London on each occasion. Two other companies also made Fishguard a port of call on the way to or from Liverpool for varying periods: the Booth Line from South America and Portugal, from April 1908 until January 1914, and the Blue Funnel Line from Australia and South Africa, from November 1910 until March 1912. After the First World war, trans-Atlantic traffic never returned to Fishguard and the Cunard and White Star Lines' transfer from Liverpool to Southampton was a major blow to the use of the port for anything other than Irish traffic — itself greatly reduced by the 'Troubles'.

The greatest day in Fishguard's

Above: Fishguard Harbour station from the north, showing the extensive cattle pens which could accommodate 800 cattle. There were subways connecting with a gallery running below the quay, along which cattle were driven to the pens after being unloaded from the steamers. At a later date all the pens were enclosed while the lines on the right were replaced by additional pens, and the station roof canopy was also extended. The tracks on the left extended around the harbour and onto the breakwater. The twin-stacked steamer is the *Inniscarra*.

Right, upper: A very distinguished portrait of Sir James Inglis, who was the GWR's Engineer from 1892 to 1904. In 1903 he was appointed General Manager, but also retained his original appointment as Engineer for the first year! In addition to the magnificent new works at Fishguard, he was also responsible as Engineer for much of the work on the new lines to South Wales, via Badminton, and to the West of England, via Westbury. As General Manager, his many notable achievements included the introduction of what became known as the 'Cornish Riviera Express'. Worn out with the pressures of his work, and by inter-departmental strife among the GWR's Chief Officers, he died very suddenly in December 1911.

Right, below: A deck view on board the GWR tender *Smeaton*, heading out to meet the *Mauretania*, on August 30 1909, with some of the many Company staff who were involved in the notable exercise. The company includes two Station Masters, five Ticket Collectors, an Inspector and the District Superintendent.

history as a harbour was August 30, 1909, when the famous *Mauretania* (holder of the Blue Riband for the fastest Atlantic crossing, for more than 20 years) made her first call to land mails and passengers from the United States. Mr. C. Aldington, Assistant Superintendent of the Line, and Mr. J.B. Morris of the Publicity Department went to New York to travel across in the liner, while Sir James Inglis, the GWR General Manager, went into residence at the Company's Fishguard Bay Hotel several days before the expected arrival; and the Company Chairman, Viscount Churchill, crossed to Ireland, and both men joined the *Mauretania* when she set down mails at Queenstown. The arrangements at Fishguard were organised to the last detail. High cliffs sheltering the west of the harbour also prevented any sight of the sea approaches from the station, so a 'look-out' was mounted on Strumble Head, in telephone communication with the Harbour Master and the station. The moment news was received that the *Mauretania* was in sight, three steamers put off from the quay to meet the mighty ship.

Above: The mighty *Mauretania* is moored off Fishguard, shortly after dropping anchor at 1.15pm on August 30 1909. The GWR tender *Smeaton* is already alongside and the *Great Western* is rounding the stern to take up position on the starboard side. The *Mauretania* (gross tonnage 31,938) was launched in September 1906 and completed in October 1907 for Cunard's trans-Atlantic service, which it shared with the same Company's *Berengaria* and *Aquitania*. The *Mauretania* was regally appointed and just two years old at the time of her Fishguard visit; she attracted much publicity and prestige for the GWR. In an age of jet travel and space exploration it is perhaps difficult to appreciate today just how important these mighty ocean liners were to the Edwardian age. The *Mauretania* retained her title as the world's fastest liner until 1929, after which the Great Depression brought hard times for her kind. Many ships were scrapped and their owners vanished, but *Mauretania* survived for a few more years, though in a much less prestigious role. She was painted white and used only for leisure cruises until, in late 1934, she sailed home for the last time. The *SS Mauretania* was sold on April 2 1935 and in the following July she sailed — under her own power — from Southampton to Rosyth, Scotland, where stripped of her fine panelling, marble fitments and luxurious furniture, she was scrapped.

Above: The GWR's *Smeaton* is tethered to the port side of the *Mauretania*, whilst mailbags from America are slid down a chute to the aft deck, as passengers disembark from the liner via a gangplank. A small steam launch is just passing the *Mauretania's* towering bow.

Above: A view from the upper deck of the *Smeaton* as the mail bags pile up for sorting and stowing in the wicker pens. Astern is the tender *Sir Francis Drake* on which the majority of passengers travelled — the *Smeaton* being responsible chiefly for the mails. Within a few minutes of completion of unloading and disembarkation, the *Mauretania* weighed anchor and resumed her voyage to Liverpool, leaving the mails and passengers at Fishguard to travel to London on GWR special trains. By the time the liner's passengers stepped ashore on the banks of the River Mersey, the Fishguard passengers were already at Paddington, where the mails arrived at 6.40pm, followed by the second of the two passenger trains at 8.00pm.

Above, right: The *Mauretania* at anchor off Fishguard, with the GWR's cargo steamer *Great Western* on the left (*Mauretania's* starboard) and *Smeaton* in attendance on the right (*Mauretania's* port).

Right, upper: Carrying Post Office staff and numerous Company servants, the *Smeaton* nears the harbour quayside at Fishguard, having unloaded 800 mail bags at the Ocean Quay (used for goods traffic) in the background. Note the locomotive-type bell whistle mounted adjacent to the 'W' of the GWR lettering on the funnel and the long vertical pipe on its left, which carried steam from the boiler safety valves.

Right, below: *Sir Francis Drake*, crowded with passengers, follows the *Smeaton* into the harbour and towards the quay. The GWR's shipping flag flies proudly from her masthead, but unlike the other tender there is no large advertisement proclaiming that the Great Western Railway is the 'Royal Mail route to London'. This vessel also has an enclosed wheelhouse (compared with the completely unprotected bridge of the *Smeaton*) and in front of the funnel is mounted a large 'organ pipe' whistle, accompanied (on the right) by a steam siren.

Left: The largest of the three GWR vessels which went out to meet the *Mauretania* was the *Great Western*, one of the Company's cargo steamers, used to carry passengers' luggage. Once again, the flying bridge is completely unprotected against the elements. The Master and his officers must have been a hardy breed! The *Smeaton, Sir Francis Drake* and *Great Western* were all summoned from GWR duties at Plymouth for the *Mauretania's* visit.

Above: Three special trains (one for mails only) were run in connection with this historic first call of the *Mauretania*, all being hauled by double-framed 4—4—0s and running non-stop to Cardiff where a trio of 'Star' 4—6—0s took over for the non-stop runs to London. The first of the passenger specials is seen leaving Fishguard Harbour station in the charge of 'City' class No.3402 *Halifax* (of Cardiff shed), which was a rebuilt 'Atbara', and 'Flower' class engine No.4108 *Gardenia* which was then only a year old. Who was the gent with the knee breeches and straw 'boater'? — he doesn't appear to be a Company servant, despite walking nonchalantly along the tracks, in full view of the signalman!

The first rail departure from Fishguard on the occasion of *Mauretania's* visit on August 30 1909 was an Ocean Mails special to Paddington seen here passing the Harbour station signalbox in the charge of 'Athara' 4—4—0 No.3381 *Maine*. The train had started from the Ocean Quay station (half-mile beyond the Harbour station) at 2.08pm — just 53 minutes after the liner dropped anchor. The first vehicle behind the tender appears to be one of four carriages built in 1904, especially for Ocean Mails duties. *Maine* hauled the five-vehicle train on the first section of the 261-miles journey to Paddington, as far as Cardiff, where 3 vehicles were detached and No. 4023 *King George* took over.

PLYMOUTH was the main Ocean Mail port served by the GWR, though in addition to the Fishguard Ocean Mail specials, the Company also ran such trains to and from Avonmouth for some years, in connection with the West Indian traffic. Fierce competition from Plymouth with the LSWR during the early 1900s resulted in the 'racing trains' to London, and also in the 'record of records' run on May 9 1904 when the 4-4-0 No. 3440 *City of Truro* became the first engine in the world to reach 100 mph, it is claimed.

As at Fishguard, the liners dropped passengers and mail a mile or so offshore at Plymouth, mail 'tenders' being used to ferry them to the quayside and the waiting train. The GWR was then exclusively concerned with the carrying of the mails, passenger traffic being the responsibility of the LSWR. The boards on the rails of the upper decks of the GWR 'tenders' bore the same legend as those at Fishguard — 'Great Western Railway, Royal Mail Route to London'.

PLYMOUTH

The transfer after the First World War of the Cunard and White Star Lines' operations from Liverpool to Southampton brought increased Ocean Mail specials and boat trains between Millbay Docks and Paddington, as the Southern Railway never attempted to recover the traffic which had once passed over the LSWR route to London. Despite the absence of any competition, the GWR continued to set up record after record in the 1920s in connection with this traffic — often in connection with the sailings of the record-breaking *SS Mauretania*. This vessel's record crossing of the Atlantic in 4 days, 21 hours and 57 minutes, saw the Ocean Mail special hauled by No. 4078 *Pembroke Castle* running from Millbay Docks Station to Paddington in 3 hours 57 minutes. On the occasion of the first call of the *SS Berengaria* at Plymouth, 'Star' 4-6-0 No. 4034 *Queen Adelaide* took only 4 hours 3 minutes to reach London, despite checks.

The Cunard Line was most appreciative of the efforts being made in connection with its fast eastbound runs, and in November 1924 the *Cunard Magazine* had this comment: "The Great Western Railway have deserved congratulations on the admirable way in which they have backed up the record-breaking runs of the big Cunarders into Plymouth. To complete the journey from Plymouth to London in under four hours is not only gratifying to the railway company concerned, but should set an example in other directions. Coming up from Southampton to London on several occasions recently — a distance of 79 miles — the journey has taken two hours. If accomplished at the same rate as the Great Western boat trains, it should have taken under 85 minutes". Possibly the fact that Ernest Cunard was also a Director of the GWR ought to be taken into account when considering these fulsome words of praise!

Right: A *Mauretania* boat train hauled by a 'Castle' 4—6—0 passes North Road station, Plymouth on September 16 1924, en route to Paddington. On this occasion, the 227 mile-journey was accomplished in 4hr 3min — at that time a new record, which featured maximum speeds in excess of 80mph. Millbay level crossing was passed at 6.25pm and arrival at Paddington was at 10.28pm.

Left: In 1924, the year of the ASLEF strike, there was also a labour stoppage at Millbay Docks, in Plymouth, leading to the use of volunteers, as shown here, to carry mails from the GWR tenders to the waiting train. Normally a conveyor belt was used to deliver mailbags directly into the vans through wide double doors. The vehicle shown here is a Churchward Ocean Mail van, fitted with six-wheel bogies.

Above: In April 1926, 300 American hotel proprietors arrived in England on the French liner *France* for a tour of this country, prior to leaving for Paris. They were given a civic welcome in Plymouth before travelling to London on a special train which reached Paddington in 3hr 53min. The 'Castle' is thought to be No.4084 *Aberystwyth Castle* (of Laira shed), seen here leaving Millbay Docks station, Plymouth. No.4084 was withdrawn from service in October 1960 and scrapped at Swindon Works the following month.

Right: The GWR scored another 'first' in connection with the *SS Mauretania* on June 19 1929, when the first Pullman Car train with ocean liner passengers from New York to London ran from Millbay Docks to Paddington. The train is seen here arriving at Paddington in the charge of No.6009 *King Charles II* — which had the unique distinction of being the only 'King' to spend it's entire life at the same shed (Old Oak Common) — this was rare for any GWR locomotive. No.6009 was withdrawn in September 1962 and scrapped in December of the same year at Cashmore's yard, Newport.

BOUND FOR
EGYPT & IRAQ

Above: An overseas connection of a very different kind, as a draft of 1,000 RAF officers and men leave Uxbridge (Vine Street) bound for Egypt and Iraq, in September 1926. The station is a fine example of a Brunel overall wooden roof terminus. Note the young boy on the left, happily in charge of what appears to be a sales tray.

Left: Farewell to friends: the forces special leaves Uxbridge (Vine Street), hauled by an 0—6—0PT. The passenger service from Vine Street to West Drayton & Yiewsley was withdrawn on September 10 1962. The train is comprised of 46ft third class non-corridor clerestory coaches designed by Dean of which 212 examples were built between 1894 and 1902.

THE
GWR/LNWR LOCOMOTIVE EXCHANGE OF 1910

Above: A stranger at Paddington — LNWR two-cylinder 'Experiment' 4—6—0 No.1471 *Worcestershire* stands at No.1 platform, ready to depart for the West of England. However, the train is probably not the 'Cornish Riviera Express', for the first carriage is a clerestory vehicle not yet repainted in the overall brown livery adopted by the GWR in 1908. Introduced in 1905, the Whale 'Experiment' 4—6—0s were a larger version of the 'Precursor' 4—4—0 of 1904. A total of 105 'Experiments' played an important role in LNWR Anglo-Scottish passenger services in the 1905-22 period.

THE early years of this century saw a number of locomotive exchanges between several of the old companies, with the LNWR participating in these to a greater extent than any other company. For example, the celebrated Caledonian 4-6-0 *Cardean* was tested against LNWR 'Experiment' 4-6-0 No. 2630 *Buffalo* between Carlisle and Crewe, whilst sister 'Experiment' No. 1405 *City of Manchester* went 'north of the border' to run between Carlisle and Glasgow, in 1909. A 'Precursor' 4-4-0 also ran in competition with one of the Great Northern Railway's Ivatt large-boilered 'Atlantics' and another 'Precursor', No. 7 *Titan*, worked between Rugby and Brighton during a comparative trial with London Brighton & South Coast superheated 4-4-2T No. 23. All these trials were initiated at the instance of C.J. Bowen-Cooke, the Chief Mechanical Engineer of the LNWR.

However, a further trial between the LNWR 'Experiment' class inside-cylinder 4-6-0 and the GWR's four-cylinder 'Star' came about in a highly distinctive fashion.

Some of the GWR's Directors had apparently become uneasy at what they regarded as the high cost of building Churchward's express passenger 4-6-0s, compared with those which the LNWR built at Crewe, details of which appear to have been obtained from one of the latter company's Board. GWR General Manager Sir James Inglis became interested and involved, as there had already been considerable disagreement between Churchward and himself. The climax came when Churchward was asked to explain to the Board why the LNWR could build three of its engines for the cost of two of those built at Swindon. His reported reply was brief and to the

Polished to gleaming perfection, Churchward four-cylinder 'Star' 4—6—0 No.4005 *Polar Star* stands beneath the unmistakeable overall roof at the LNWR's London terminus, at Euston, in 1910. The 225lbs per square inch (psi) boiler pressure of the 'Stars' (and all Churchward's other main line engines) was considerably higher than the 175psi working pressure of the majority of LNWR locomotives, giving the GWR locomotive a distinct advantage in the 1910 Exchange. Crewe's only four-cylinder 4—6—0s of that period (Webb's Compound mixed traffic engines of the '1400' class) had 200psi boilers, they were not particularly successful in traffic and all were withdrawn within 20 years of construction. The LNWR 'Experiment' 4—6—0s were withdrawn between 1925 and 1935; the majority of the GWR 'Stars' remained in service and hard at work for nearly 40 years.

point: "Because one of mine could pull two of their b★★★★y things backwards!" His bold claim was subsequently put to the test in the interchange trials of August 1910, when the loads of the West of England expresses were at their peak.

If Churchward had anticipated the outcome of the trials with assurance, the reverse must have been true as far as Bowen-Cooke and his colleagues at Crewe were concerned. Their fears were not without foundation, for the disparity between Churchward's superb four-cylinder 'Star', with its long-travel valve gear, and the much smaller two-cylinder 'Experiment' was made very clear indeed in the trials. Although the first of the GWR's four-cylinder engines, No. 40 (later No. 4000 *North Star*) emerged from Swindon only 11 months after the first of the LNWR's 'Experiments' had entered traffic, they represented very different phases in the development of the steam locomotive.

On the West Coast main line between Euston and Crewe, the GWR's No. 4005 *Polar Star* handled the expresses with ease during the trials in competition with 'Experiment'

No. 1455 *Hertfordshire*, but it was on the GWR West of England line that the absolute superiority of the Swindon engine was demonstrated. The visiting LNWR engine was No. 1471 *Worcestershire*, of Camden shed, and the choice of this particular engine appears to have been dictated by the fact that it had covered 45,000 miles since it was last 'shopped' and could be most readily spared at the height of the busy summer holiday season! 'Playing at home' on this occasion was No. 4003 *Lode Star*, and once again there was little or no comparison in the performance of the rivals.

On the first trip with the 'Cornish Riviera Express' *Worcestershire* was 33 minutes late at Plymouth, and performance went from bad to worse on successive days. For her size she was grossly overloaded. On August 24 *Worcestershire* ran on the 11.50am service to Exeter, with the dynamometer car attached: the initial load was 415 tons, reduced successively to 385 tons after Westbury and 270 tons from Taunton by the release of slip carriages, and Exeter was reached 13½ mins. late.

Ironically, it has since been estab-

lished that the building cost of an 'Experiment' was around £3,123; while the GWR's 'Stars' averaged £3,200 each. One suspects that the LNWR figure quoted to a GWR Director was either far from accurate - or far from truthful! We shall never know which, but the trials of August 1910 certainly gave Churchward's engines a chance to shine.

Below: *Worcestershire* **leaves Paddington, bound for the west of England. The LNWR 'Experiment' was a much smaller engine than the GWR 'Star', and there was the additional handicap of limited coal and water capacity, for** *Worcestershire* **carried just six tons of coal and 3,000 gallons of water, compared with the Swindon 4—6—0's capacity of seven tons of coal and 3,500 gallons of water. Also, whereas the 'Star' was designed for non-stop running between Paddington and Plymouth (225 miles) the 'Experiments' had been built primarily for the Crewe-Carlisle section (141 miles) of the LNWR's Anglo-Scottish West Coast Main Line. It was therefore hardly surprising that Churchward's 'Star' fared rather better than Whale's 'Experiment' in the GWR/LNWR locomotive exchange of August 1910.**

THE GWR AT

LONDON VICTORIA

COMPARATIVELY few people probably know that the GWR once had a second London terminus — at Victoria! The GWR reached Victoria by means of the West London Extension Railway over which broad gauge rails were laid for their convenience, though the service which commenced between Victoria and Southall also had some 'narrow gauge' GWR trains, and by October 1866 the service became wholly standard gauge. At Victoria, the Company joined with the newly-arrived London, Chatham & Dover Railway in leasing half of the new station, which had been built by the Victoria Station & Pimlico Company. The service between Victoria and Southall lasted for many years and connected with some main line trains at Ealing.

It was not until 1910 that the GWR attempted to make use of Victoria Station where its name was displayed on the outer walls below that of the

Top: A GWR train from Wolverhampton and Birmingham runs into Victoria station, in 1910, hauled by 'Atbara' 4—4—0 No.3384 *Omdurman*. All the carriages are of the clerestory type. William Dean's 40 'Atbara' 4—4—0s, built in 1900 and 1901 had 6ft 8in driving wheels and were capable of running at a sustained speed of 75mph with up to six coaches over a level road. They were popular and successful but the days of the double-framed 4—4—0 as front line power were numbered, especially after Churchward started developing the 4—6—0. Nevertheless, the express passenger 4—4—0s remained at work for a long time: 'Atbara' withdrawals did not start until 1927, and the class was extinct by 1931.

Above: A view of the train shown at the top of the page, standing at Victoria, showing a carriage destination board, which reads: 'VICTORIA (S.E. & C. AND G.W.) BIRMINGHAM & WOLVERHAMPTON VIA THE NEW ROUTE'. The coach — the end vehicle of the up train — is a brake third. The group of SECR platform staff includes an Inspector, on the right.

Right: The train ready to depart from Victoria, clearly showing clerestory brake third class coach No. 2338, which is painted in the all-over brown livery used by the GWR from 1908 until 1912. Crimson Lake was used thereafter for carriages until 1922, when the 'traditional' chocolate and cream was reintroduced. *Omdurman* was built in July 1900, fitted with a taper boiler in April 1910, superheated in June 1912, fitted with piston valves in December 1915, and eventually withdrawn in April 1930.

Above: Having run round its train, No. 3384 departs tender first from Victoria from beneath the distinctive arched roof. When built, Victoria was leased in perpetuity jointly to the GWR and the London Chatham & Dover Railway, and whilst GWR usage of the station lasted only from April 1 1863 to March 22 1915, this lease remained in force after the Grouping. After 1923 the Southern Railway, as freeholder, continued to receive rent from the GWR in return both for GWR authority to use South Eastern & Chatham Railway for other than local trains. However, the opening of the new, direct route between Paddington and Birmingham, via Bicester, was followed by the Victoria, and the right to be consulted regarding proposed alterations and improvements. In 1933, agreement was reached whereby the GWR surrendered all rights to Victoria, apart from limited running powers, in return for abolition of the rent payments. This gave the SR total control at Victoria. A rear three-quarter view of this nature highlights the very spartan protection provided for the footplate crew by the rather meagre GWR cabs of this era. introduction of a through service between Victoria, Birmingham and Wolverhampton. This unlikely venture was the result of the intense competition which had developed between the GWR and the LNWR, with the latter company running a train between Broad Street and Birmingham to attract the custom of businessmen.

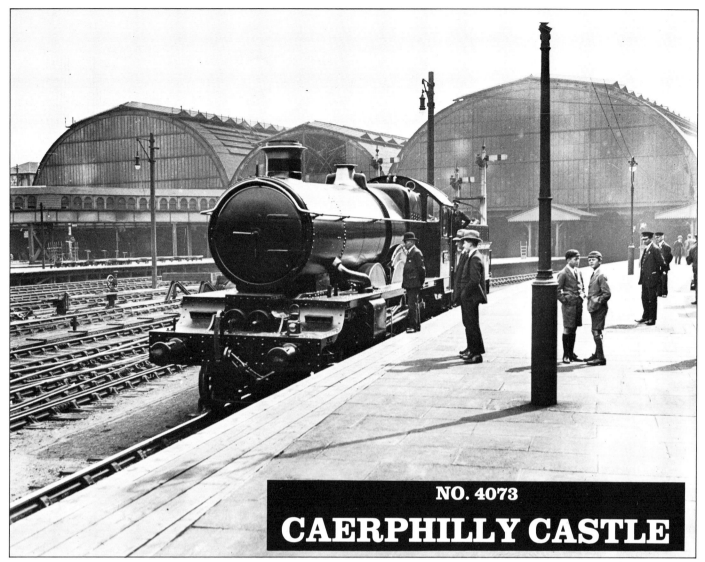

CAERPHILLY CASTLE

CHURCHWARD'S 'Stars' were undoubtedly the most outstanding express passenger locomotives in Britain prior to the Grouping, and they were handling the GWR's heaviest express workings without difficulty. However, something larger and more powerful was required for the future, especially as longer and heavier trains were going to be needed to deal with the increasing West of England holiday traffic. Consequently, in August 1923 the GWR announced that: "the most powerful express passenger engine in Great Britain" had emerged from Swindon Works — No.4073 *Caerphilly Castle*. The new locomotive was in all respects an enlarged 'Star', having four 16in (diameter) and 26in (stroke) cylinders (compared with those of 15in diameter on the 'Star') and a larger boiler whose firebox had a grate area of 30.28 sq.ft, compared with it's predecessor's 27.07 sq.ft. Both classes had a boiler pressure of 225psi, which had been standard on the GWR

for the largest tender engines since 1903.

The most obvious external differences between the 'Star' and the 'Castle' were the provision of a larger cab with side windows, and the fitting of curved external steam pipes to the outside cylinders. The diagonal rain strip on the cab roof was not fitted to any other example, and was soon removed — as were the bogie brakes fitted to the first ten 'Castles', which perpetuated what had been a standard Churchward practice on all 4—6—0s and on the outside cylinder 4—4—0s of the 'County' class. *Caerphilly Castle* was also fully lined out, even below the footplate, and heralded a much-welcomed return to what had been the GWR livery for express pasenger engines prior to the war years.

The 'Castles' were immediately successful and a total of 171 were built, the last examples rolling out of Swindon Works in 1950, under the auspices of British Railways (Western

Above: *Caerphilly Castle* **was soon sent to Paddington for inspection by the Directors — and to be admired by the public! In this scene, in August 1923, two young enthusiasts can be seen discussing the latest result of Swindon's famous 'Wiltshire Wisdom', while a bowler-hatted Locomotive Inspector studies the inside motion, and several uniformed staff admire the new locomotive.**

Region). They were economical, fast and extremely popular with footplate crews. The GWR was extremely proud of its new creation, and the Company's Publicity Department went to work with great vigour, and a considerable degree of success. A special book about *Caerphilly Castle* was published by the GWR, and within a single month in 1924, no fewer than 40,000 copies were printed. The 'Castles' performed with great success on front line passenger duties until the last days of steam traction on the Western Region, as a fine tribute to GWR motive power design.

Above: An official photograph of No.4073 *Caerphilly Castle*, painted in works grey livery. Althogh physically smaller than Gresley's contemporary 'Pacifics', in terms of calculated tractive effort Collett's 'Castle' was the more powerful, with a rating of 31,625lbs, compared with the 29,835lbs accorded to the LNER 4—6—2s. This enabled the GWR's, Publicity Department to label the 'Castle' as Britain's most powerful express passenger steam locomotive; this was based in wholly notional and theoretical calculation, but it allowed the GWR to give the 'Castle' some of the best and most enduring publicity ever accorded to a steam locomotive.

Above: The Locomotive Inspector pays attention to the cab, whose diagonal rain strip on the roof is clearly visible, but the attention of the young enthusiasts appears to have been distracted. Only *Caerphilly Castle* was fitted with this rain-strip, which was designed to divert rain water to drip into the tender, rather than onto the crew. The first 'Castles' were paired with low-sided 3,500-gallon tenders, as seen here, the more familiar high-sided 4,000-gallon type not being introduced until 1926. The old style tender looks rather incongruous with the more modern cab, which was described thus by W.A. Tuplin: "...joking apart, the 'Castle' cab was an advance in Swindon practice. One could say that the enginemen were 'in the cab' and not just 'on the footplate'!"

Left: Locomotive Inspector and Driver stand beside the new, gleaming locomotive at track level, as another young man — possibly a GWR workman — stares at the latest wonder. The reason for the distracted attention of the two young enthusiasts is now apparent (facing page, lower) in the shape of the immaculate two-cylinder 'Saint' 4—6—0 No.2904 *Lady Godiva* standing alongside platform No.2. No.2904 was the fourth of ten 4—6—0s built in May 1906 and named after 'Ladies', the first of which, No.2901 *Lady Superior*, was the first locomotive with a modern superheater (of the Schmidt firetube type) to be built and run on a railway in Britain. No.2904 was at this period shedded at Stafford Road, and was withdrawn from service (from Shrewsbury) in October 1932. Note once again the bogie brakes fitted to No.4073.

Above: The cab of No.4073 *Caerphilly Castle*, with the Locomotive Inspector, Fireman and Driver. The GWR was alone among the 'Big Four' in always retaining right-hand drive for all its engines, though this had been a common practice on many of the pre-grouping railways. The driver appears to be enjoying the comfort of a larger cab: footplate comfort was one of the few aspects of locomotive design in which the GWR could never have been credited with being in the vanguard! Visible in the left and right foreground are the curved lids of the tender tool boxes, whilst also on the left can be seen one of the 'mushroom' vents for the water tank. The two cranked handles, in front of the tool boxes operated the tender handbrake and water scoop. Immediately left of the driver can be seen the triple sight classes of the hydrostatic lubricator, above which is the vacuum brake valve and vacuum gauge. The position of the brake valve made it very difficult for the driver to operate the brake and also lean out to see where he was going — unless he had very long arms! The regulator handle is centrally placed above the firehole, with the single gauge glass (to show the boiler water level) on it's left. The chain was used to 'flick' the flap into the firehole.

Below: No. 4073 *Caerphilly Castle* makes a highly characteristic aggressive departure from Paddington in the Autumn of 1924, following it's return to service after the British Empire Exhibition, where it was displayed by the GWR from April to October. The GWR — ever publicity conscious — had taken the 4—6—0 to Wembley within 24 hours of bringing the up 'Limited' into Paddington, to stress that this was an everyday, working locomotive and not a specially prepared exhibition piece. A board attached to *Caerphilly Castle* proclaimed it to be the country's most powerful passenger locomotive and visitors were left to ponder this point as they moved on to examine the larger LNER 'Pacific' No.4472 *Flying Scotsman*, which was displayed on an adjacent stand. Comparisons made between the two locomotives led to the famous 'exchange' of April-May 1925, when a 'Castle' ran on the East Coast Main Line from King's Cross, and a Gresley 'Pacific' worked from Paddington to the West of England.

Right: A station porter awaits a 'clear road' of his own as No.4073 *Caerphilly Castle* is seen again in September 1936. The apertures in the frames ahead of the outside cylinders (to allow access to the inside valve motion) can clearly be seen. It was the valve gear, combined with the superb tapered Churchward boiler which gave the GWR such a lead in the matter of express passenger power: the LMS and LNER were relative 'latecomers' to long-travel valve gear, as used by the GWR, but Maunsell, on the Southern Railway, had been aware of the advantages, and had used long travel valves on his 'N' class 'Moguls', designed for the South Eastern & Chatham Railway during the war years.

ROYAL VISIT
TO
SWINDON WORKS

ON April 28 1924 the GWR was honoured by a royal visit to Swindon Works by Their Royal Highnesses King George V and Queen Mary, who were escorted by the GWR Chairman Viscount Churchill, and Vice Chairman Sir Ernest Palmer, as well as by Mr. C.B. Collett, the Chief Mechanical Engineer, General Manager Sir Felix J. Pole, and Works Managers E.T.J. Evans (Carriage & Wagon) and R.A.C. Hannington (Locomotive). This was only the second time that King George V and Queen Mary had visited a locomotive works, the first visit having been to the LNWR's works at Crewe, in 1913.

Above: Touring the engine yard, Her Royal Highness Queen Mary is walking between Sir Ernest Palmer (left) and Mr. Collett, whilst a few steps behind, His Majesty King George V is escorted by Viscount Churchill. Directly behind the Mayor, and wearing a wing collar, bowler hat and moustache is William Stanier, then Collett's Assistant on the GWR. A large crowd of workmen are watching the royal entourage from the workshop roof. The locomotive on the left is No. 181, an 0—6—2T acquired by the GWR when it took over the working of the Rhondda & Swansea Bay Railway in July 1906, though it retained its RSB number (No. 4) until the company was absorbed in 1922. Built by Kitson in 1885, the locomotive was one of the earliest engines of the 0—6—2T type in South Wales, an area which subsequently became particularly associated with engines of that wheel arrangement: 422 of the 731 engines acquired by the GWR from the various South Wales railways were 0—6—2Ts! As seen here, No.181 carries a boiler with which it had been rebuilt at Swindon in 1908. The other tank engine on the left is one of the 'large Metro' 2—4—0Ts, which for many years handled the majority of the GWR's suburban workings in the London area.

Left: His Royal Highness King George V uses a screen whilst watching "quasi-arc electrical welding" in the Works. The Mayor of Swindon, Alderman T.C. Newman (for once, Swindon did not have a 'railway' Mayor that year!), can be seen in the background. The bowler-hatted gentleman accompanying the King is C.B. Collett, the GWR's Chief Mechanical Engineer, from 1922 to 1941.

After arriving at Swindon on the GWR's royal train, HRH King George V and HRH Queen Mary motored to the Works, where they were met by CME C.B. Collett and his Assistant, William Stanier, together with Carriage & Wagon Works Manager E.T.J. Evans. The royal visitors had expressed a wish to see the Works in operation and meet members of the workforce and the GWR was pleased to comply, as illustrated by the accompanying photographs, produced by the Topical Press Agency.

In the Carriage & Wagon Works, the King and Queen visited the Carriage Works' Finishing and Trimming Shops, Body-Making Shops, Polishing and Finishing Shops and the Saw Mill, whilst in the Locomotive Works, the royal visitors toured the Iron Foundry, the Test Plant, the General Machine Shop, the Engine Erecting Shop, the Wheel Shop and the Weighbridge. A complete locomotive was lifted by overhead crane and a further locomotive was turned on a turntable, for demonstration purposes. At the conclusion of the visit, the King drove No. 4082 *Windsor Castle* from the Works to Swindon station, where the royal train was waiting, for the return trip to Windsor. Thereafter, No. 4082 became the regular royal train engine.

The GWR Works was established at Swindon in 1842, and grew steadily over the years to service the ever-increasing demands of the busy system. The Works was closed by British Rail Engineering Ltd in March 1986, but at the time of the royal visit of 1924, the workshops occupied 310 acres — including 65 acres of roofed accommodation. In 1924, 7,500 men were employed in the Locomotive Works, in the fitting, erecting and machine shops, the iron and brass foundries and the boilersmiths, tinsmiths and other metalwork shops. Around 1,000 locomotives a year passed through Swindon for repair, in addition to which the Works was capable of producing two brand new locomotives each week.

The biggest workshop was the famous 'A' shop, which occupied half a million square feet of floor area, and at the time of the royal visit was equipped with a quartet of 100-ton capacity travelling cranes, of 75ft span. The GWR was particularly renowned for its quite superb range of standard locomotive boilers, and the Works boiler shop was well equipped to meet the needs of the post-war GWR. Rivetting was accomplished by pneumatic machinery, whilst

Above: Whilst visiting the Iron Foundry, the King and Queen examine a mould used to cast a personal greeting for the royal couple. This message still adorned the wall of what later became the No. 9 shop until the closure of Swindon Works in March 1986.

At the time of the royal visit of 1924, GWR Chairman Viscount Churchill had an aide-memoir of facts prepared, and the following 'round' figures for Swindon were:

No. of employees at the CME's Department, Swindon	14,000
No. of women employees at Swindon	400
Wages bill (per annum)	£2,500,000
Costs were quoted as follows:	
Express passenger locomotive	£6,700
70ft Dining Car	£4,600
70ft First Class Carriage	£3,500
70ft Third Class Carriage	£3,000
20 ton mineral wagon	£240
12 ton mineral wagon	£165

hydraulic presses were used for flanging and bending steel tubeplates and copper firebox plates. Extensive use was made throughout the Works of acetylene and electric welding techniques, and forward progress was encouraged by the work of the chemical laboratory, research department and the stationary test plant, which was then unique in this country.

The Carriage & Wagon Works employed a further 5,600 men in 1924, working in the saw mill and the workshops devoted to body construction, repair, finishing, painting, trimming, wheels, and smithy work. In a year, the workforce was capable of repairing 5,000 carriages, of which 3,000 required major attention, whilst at the same time constructing 200 new vehicles of various types. In the wagon works, the annual throughput for repair was 8,000 vehicles per annum, whilst the new construction limit was about

4,500 vehicles per year. Timber was made ready for use in rolling stock construction by artificially accelerated seasoning, in special drying sheds. The Works generated its own electricity and manufactured its own gas in a plant capable of producing three million cubic feet of gas every 24 hours. In 1924, this gas plant was the largest privately-owned installation of its kind in the world.

As indicated in the accompanying table of statistics, women were not extensively employed in the works; apart from a few machinists, women worked mainly in the laundry, sewing shops and polishing shops. In the laundry the workforce handled towels, antimaccassars, dusters and a host of other items, and in 1923 more than 2½ million items were cleaned and returned to use.

In addition to locomotive, carriage and wagon work, Swindon Works also provided points and crossings used by the Permanent Way

Left: The tour of the Carriage Works included a visit to the sawmills, where the royal visitors have witnessed the slicing of a tree trunk (probably of Baltic Oak) into planks for use in carriage construction. By this time the GWR was building steel-panelled stock - unlike the LMS which continued to build wooden-bodied carriages until 1929. The electricity for the sawmill was produced by a generator powered by a gas engine, the fuel for which came from a gas suction plant fed by mill refuse.

Below: The highlight which concluded the royal visit of 1924 was the invitation to the King to drive the new 'Castle' class engine No. 4082 *Windsor Castle* from the works to Swindon station, this engine having worked the royal train from Paddington. In addition to the King and Queen, the driver and the fireman, there was also Viscount Churchill, Sir Felix J. Pole, Mr. Collett and Chief Locomotive Inspector George Flewellyn. The enginemen, Driver E. Rowe and Fireman A. Cook (both of Old Oak Common shed), made history a year later with their magnificent running on No. 4074 *Caldicot Castle* during the interchange trials with the LNER. On the occasion of the royal visit they received a letter of thanks, a copy of the souvenir programme, and bonuses of £2 and £1 respectively. In this picture, Collett is waiting anxiously for the royal couple, clutching a number of handcloths for the VIPs.

Department, and large numbers of castings required for signalling and telegraph work. To list the total contribution of the Works to the GWR system would be a lengthy task however, for there were few aspects of life on the GWR which did not benefit to a greater or lesser extent from equipment and tools manufactured in the huge works at Swindon.

Comparative construction costs (per locomotive) for successive GWR express passenger classes:

1906: Four-cylinder 4—4—2 No. 40 (subsequently rebuilt as 4—6—0 No. 4000,
the first 'Star') £3,218
1922: Final lot of 'Stars', Nos. 4061-4072 .... £7,516*f*
1924: First lot of 'Castles', Nos. 4073-82 .... £5,565
1927: First lot of 'Kings', Nos. 6000-6019 .... £6,383
1930: Second lot of 'Kings', Nos. 6020-6029 .... £6,172
1932: Fourth lot of 'Castles', Nos. 5013-5022 .... £5,190

f This high cost was as a result of post-First World War inflation.

In each instance, the cost of the tender is not included; however, the tenders for the 'King' class 4—6—0s cost an average of £1,001 to construct.

A NEW APPROACH TO COAL

THE inclusion of the cost of a 20-ton mineral wagon (£240) among the comparative figures quoted by the GWR's Chairman on the occasion of the Royal Visit to Swindon Works (see page 67) was significant. The GWR had just introduced a new design of 20-ton coal wagon and was actively engaged in attempting to persuade the South Wales collieries to change over to using these vehicles in place of the traditional 10-ton capacity wagons. The campaign included a special demonstration of the advantages of such wagons, arranged not only for the benefit of the colliery owners and management, but also for the press. This demonstration, illustrated here, was staged at Severn Tunnel Junction on August 26, 1924.

Incentives to use the new wagons were stated to be: the saving of about 30% in siding space, thus eliminating the need to lay down extra sidings at collieries; appreciable savings in capital outlay compared with the purchase of smaller wagons and finally, an offer of a 5% rebate off conveyance rates on coal carried in fully-loaded 20 ton wagons! Ironically, the miners' strike in 1926 and the great trade depression of the late 1920s meant that many collieries had more than enough sidings, while coal traffic on the GWR decreased dramatically. In 1928 it fell by nearly 3 million tons and there was a loss of revenue of more than £300,000 at the docks alone, apart from conveyance charges. In 1913, coal exports in South Wales had amounted to 39 million tons: in 1928 this had declined to 26½ million tons.

Above: On the right is one of the new 20-ton all-steel wagons, which had end doors for use when tipping coal into hopper shutes at the docks, contrasted with a 10-ton capacity typical private owner coal wagon owned by Bradbury's — who were among the first users of the new wagons.

Below: One of Churchward's incomparable heavy freight engines, No. 2807, heads a train of the new wagons. The 2-8-0 type was introduced into this country by the GWR in 1903, and by 1919 there were 84 of these powerful engines in use. No. 2807 was rebuilt with outside steam pipes in November 1936 and was withdrawn, from Severn Tunnel Junction, in March 1963: it is one of five engines of this type which have been preserved, and is based at the Gloucestershire Warwickshire Railway.

Above: Another view of No. 2807 and its 1,000-ton train — at least, the load would have been 1,000 tons had the wagons been full. However, the train is heading west and the wagons are destined for delivery to North's Navigation Colliery, Maesteg. The first 500 wagons were to be utilised for shipment of coal at Port Talbot and Swansea (King's Dock) while others were shortly to be introduced at Newport Docks. 950 of the new wagons were ordered, built as follows: 200 at Swindon, 250 by the Gloucester Carriage & Wagon Co. Ltd., 250 by the Birmingham Carriage & Wagon Co. Ltd. and 250 by the Bute Works Supply Co. Ltd. and Stableford & Co. Ltd.

Above: Contrasting with the 'new look', a train formed of the smaller wooden-bodied private owners' wagons, many of them owned by Bradbury. The train may have been typical of such traffic, but the motive power was not: the 'Metro' class 2—4—0T must have had some difficulty with such a load, and a more typical engine for such traffic, a 2-8-0T, can be seen at the head of the train on the right.

Right: A Churchward 'Mogul' heads another train of the new wagons passing through Severn Tunnel Junction on delivery, in August 1924. To illustrate the operational advantages of the new large capacity wagons, a demonstration train of 50 10-ton wagons was marshalled at Severn Tunnel Junction, its length being 1,009ft. A train of 50 20-ton wagons was 1,225ft long, with a capacity of 1,000-tons, giving a 396ft saving in length on 500 tons of coal. A hire scheme was offered, whereby the new wagons could be hired at 13s 4d per wagon per week over an eight-year period. This was to assist colliery owners who were unable to afford buying a new fleet of wagons. Although laudable in principle, the scheme to spread the use of 20-ton wagons met with only limited success, owing to the high cost not only of buying or hiring the wagons themselves, but also of providing suitable loading facilities. These engines, introduced in 1911 were the GWR's 'maids of all work' and hauled a wide variety of traffic from express passenger trains, in Cornwall and North of Wolverhampton, to heavy mineral traffic. They were the first general purpose engines in Britain, 322 being built between 1911 and 1925.

Above: A general view of Severn Tunnel Junction, looking towards Newport, with the up yard on the right, one of the large 2—6—2Ts of the '3150' class is marshalling a train: a number of these engines were always to be found at Severn Tunnel Junction, where their main duty was assisting heavy coal trains through 'The Hole' as the tunnel was always known. Note the single blade catch point on the loop line, also the amazing 'round the mulberry bush' point rods, from the signal box, which actually follow three sides of a square to reach the points on the left!

AS a consequence of the 1924 Wembley Exhibition when *Caerphilly Castle* and *Flying Scotsman* stood close together as if in open rivalry, there was an exchange of locomotives between the GWR and the LNER in the following year. It is still not at all clear as to how this was arranged or by whom, but it seems most likely that it was largely the work of the GWR's energetic General Manager, Felix J. Pole. It is improbable that the suggestion emanated from the LNER's Chief Mechanical Engineer, Nigel Gresley, who was reported to be displeased with news of the approaching exchange, but as the instruction came from a very senior level, the die was cast. As a consequence, No. 4079 *Pendennis Castle* spent a fortnight in April-May 1925 working between King's Cross and Doncaster, while the LNER's Pacific No. 4474 *Victor Wild* worked the 'Cornish Riviera Express' between Paddington and Plymouth. *Pendennis Castle* is seen here leaving the suburban platforms King's Cross on April 22 1925, on a stopping train to Peterborough, during the pre-test week when Driver Young and his mate were 'learning the road.'

Although the LNER's Driver Pibworth performed most commendably with *Victor Wild* over the much more difficult line between Paddington and Plymouth, there can

be no doubt that the LNER was well and truly outclassed on its own road as far as performance was concerned, the manner in which *Pendennis Castle* accelerated its train smartly out of King's Cross — as seen here — and up Holloway Bank was an 'eye opener' to many of the LNER personnel who had confidently predicted that the 'Castle' would 'stick' inside the tunnel! Indeed, in the course of the trials, *Pendennis Castle* passed Finsbury Park on each journey less than six minutes after leaving King's Cross, hauling trains of up to 480 tons loading. It is thought

that the GWR 4—6—0 thereby established a record never since beaten by an LNER 'Pacific'. The importance of adequately proportioned, long-travel valves was brought into very sharp focus for the LNER, which thereafter progressively applied these principles to its motive power fleet. The Gresley 'Pacifics', whose powerful capabilities at the head of a train had never been in doubt, became much more efficient machines as a result. No. 4079, withdrawn from service in May 1964, is now preserved in Australia.

Top: 1925 was also the Centenary Year of the Stockton & Darlington Railway, in which all of the 'Big Four' shared through their provision of locomotives and rolling stock for the exhibition and parade at Darlington. The GWR's contribution included two 'Castle' 4-6-0s and complete trains: No. 4082 Windsor Castle hauled the GWR Royal Train, while No. 111 Viscount Churchill headed a train of articulated main line carriages, vehicles usually more associated with Sir Nigel Gresley and the LNER. The GWR built 18 articulated carriages for 'Main Line and City' suburban service in June 1925, and followed these with a second articulated train intended for main line express services. The latter comprised two units of three carriages and one of two carriages, these consisting of: two third class carriages and a third class brake; third class dining carriage, kitchen car, first class dining carriage; first class carriage and first class brake. All units had 7ft bogies at the outer ends, and heavy duty 8ft 6in bogies with double pivots at the point of articulation. The stock was so new, having only emerged from Swindon Works a few days prior to travelling to Darlington, that it had almost certainly never carried any passengers! No. 111 Viscount Churchill had been reconstructed in September 1924 from Churchward's famous Pacific, The Great Bear, the first 4—6—2 to be seen in Britain and the only 'Pacific' built by the GWR. The caption originally provided for this photograph is not likely to have endeared the photographer either to Nigel Gresley or to the GWR: "GWR locomotive 111 Viscount Churchill — 1st 'Pacific' class built at Swindon from Gresley's patent. Rebuilt in 1924 from The Great Bear originally built in 1908". One wonders if this information had been provided by a 'helpful' member of the LNER staff! No. 111 was later to become one of the earlier 'Castle' withdrawals, in July 1953 (from Laira), having spent most of its life shedded at Old Oak Common.

Above: Among the modern freight locomotives in the 1925 parade was Churchward's magnificent mixed traffic 2—8—0 No. 4700, which was fully lined-out for the occasion. The nine engines of this class, built between 1919 and 1923, carried a much larger boiler than the Standard No. 1 on the 'Saints', 'Stars' and '2800' class 2—8—0s, though No. 4700 had initially carried such a boiler. No. 4700 was equipped with the Standard No. 7 boiler, which remained unique to this class. The proposal for a larger 4—6—0 which resulted in the production of the 'Castles', had included the use of this boiler, but this had to be abandoned on grounds of excessive weight. The '4700' class 2—8—0s were mainly employed on overnight fast fitted-freight workings between London and Wolverhampton, Bristol and Plymouth, though they were also used on passenger workings during the peak holiday traffic times — on which they were restricted to a maximum speed of 60 mph. They were the first GWR locomotives to have outside steam pipes. No. 4700 was withdrawn in September 1962 and subsequently stored at Southall Shed (81C) until January 1964: the locomotive was scrapped by King's of Norwich, in March of that year. No examples of the '4700' class survive.

Below: Also included in the parade was 2—8—0T No. 5225, built in May 1924 and also fully lined out for the occasion — the normal livery for such engines (as for the '4700' class) was unlined green. It also carried the old-style GWR Coat-of-Arms. The 2—8—0T was unknown in Britain, except on the GWR, where 205 examples of this type were built between 1910 and 1940, 54 of which were subsequently converted to 2—8—2Ts, with larger bunkers for main line work, between 1934 and 1939. The '4200' and '5205' classes (the latter having 19in x 30in cylinders compared with the 18½in diameter cylinders of the earlier engines) were chiefly employed on working coal trains in South Wales, though two engines were shedded at St. Blazey in Cornwall for working china clay traffic to the docks at Fowey. They were also used on banking duties at Glyn Neath. Extremely sure-footed engines, they were rarely known to slip, even when working heavy coal trains in wet weather. No. 5225 was withdrawn in August 1963. The fabulous LNER Beyer-Garratt 2—8—0+0—8—2 No. 2395 can be seen in the distance as No. 42 in the parade, preparing to run past the spectators.

Left: The final GWR exhibit was unable to take part in the parade: not only was the replica of the early broad-gauge engine *North Star* of the wrong gauge, but it was also non-working. The original *North Star* had been built by R. Stephenson & Co. in 1837 (initially for the 5ft 6in gauge New Orleans Railway) and was without doubt by far the most reliable engine in the motley collection which Daniel Gooch inherited when he took over the position of GWR Locomotive Superintendent, which was doubtless a relief to Gooch, as he had formerly worked at Stephenson's and had been largely responsible for designing the engine! Withdrawn in 1871, *North Star* was preserved at Swindon, together with Gooch's famous 8ft 'Single' *Lord of the Isles,* until February 1906 when the priceless relics were broken up because of lack of space, no museum being willing to accept them. The 1925 replica included a few parts from the original engine, including the top portion of the chimney which — it is alleged — had been used as a piano stool!

THE
GENERAL STRIKE, MAY 1926

THE widespread strike by railway staff of all departments and grades in 1919 and the ASLEF strike in 1924 were followed by the even greater disruption caused by the General Strike from May 4-14 in 1926. On May 2 Sir Felix Pole had made a bid to avoid the worst affects on the GWR, by sending a message to all stations and departments, worded as follows: "The National Union of Railwaymen have intimated that railwaymen have been asked to strike without notice tomorrow night. Each Great Western man has to decide his course of action, but I appeal to all of you to hesitate before you break your contracts of service with the old company, before you inflict grave injury upon the railway industry and before you arouse ill-feeling in the railway service which will take years to remove. Railway companies and railwaymen have demonstrated that they can settle their disputes by direct negotiations. The mining industry should be advised to do the same.

"Remember that your means of living and your personal interests are involved, and that Great Western men are trusted to be loyal to their conditions of service in the same manner as they expect the company to carry out their obligations and agreements".

At first, there was a fairly general cessation of traffic, though in the London area some 'stopping' trains worked on the main line, including one service from Oxford, stopping at all stations to Paddington. The 'Irish Mail' from Fishguard started at

Above: A local train from Slough arrives at Paddington's No. 6 platform during the General Strike, the engine — No. 2223 of the 4—4—2 'County tank' class — having been driven by "amateur footplatemen", according to the original caption. The engines of the '2221' class were a tank version of the outside cylinder 4—4—0 'County' class, hence the name by which they were commonly known, but they carried a smaller boiler. They were notable in having 6ft 8½in driving wheels, the largest coupled wheels ever used on a tank engine. The 40 engines of this class, built between 1905 and 1912, were all employed on the outer suburban services from Paddington, until displaced by 2—6—2Ts of the '6100' class during the early 1930s. Note the selection of mixed carriages standing at No. 4 platform, including a low-roofed brake vehicle fitted with side lamps, a practice which lasted until June 1 1933. The roof profiles in No. 5 platform indicates a train of very mixed stock!

76

Left: London's milk supply depended on the ability of the railways to transport it daily from far afield; in the case of the GWR, from the West of England and South Wales. There were some most unusual workings of carriage stock during the period of the General Strike, for it was not normal to find carriages carrying destination boards for 'Cardiff, Newport, Shrewsbury, Chester and Birkenhead' at Paddington! The cloth-capped men in the foreground in this view, on May 12 1926, are possibly strikers, glumly watching volunteers helping to ensure the ultimate failure of the strike.

Below: Locomotives were not the only machines to be driven by volunteers during the General Strike. The original Topical Press caption for this photograph reads: "Mrs. Talbot. Voluntary transport-driver during the General Strike". One wonders if the lady learnt to drive such vehicles as an ambulance driver during the First World War. Note the strand of barbed wire which appears to be in danger of dislodging the radiator cap, and the number plate, which seems to be partly secured in position by string! The AEC lorry carries much interesting detail — note particularly the solid-tyred spoked wheels the starting handle, towing hook, oil lamps, trumpet-type horn and the lack of cab doors or windscreen.

3.20am and worked through to London, stopping at principal and many other stations. A number of GWR men refused to strike, while increasing numbers of staff returned to work within a day or two, and assisted by many thousands of volunteers, the train service was steadily increased. Although on the first day there were only 194 trains on the GWR, by the fifth day there were 500, and this had increased to more than 1,000 by the eighth day, while on the last day no less than 1,517 trains were operated.

One remarkable feature of the General Strike was the GWR's ability not only to deal with the normal ocean passenger and mails traffic through Plymouth, but to handle additional landings diverted into that port. Seven special trains were run to London to transport 3,000 passengers landed from 20 boats; while in other cases the two trains regularly run at 9.25am and 12.30pm to Paddington were used. In addition, three embarkations were arranged, including a special call of the P&O Company's ship *Kaiser-i-Hind* for which a restaurant car special was run from Paddington! It was reckoned that within the first day or two of the strike more than 100,000 employees of the GWR were at work, though the number of volunteers who helped to maintain the train service and other vital activities does not appear to have been recorded.

Above: Goods traffic was not normally handled at Paddington's platforms, but during the General Strike essential and perishable merchandise replaced passengers, while GWR lorries and vans replaced the customary taxis. The distribution of essential supplies had been organised well in advance, once a stoppage in support of the miners had appeared increasingly likely. Both the NUR and ASLEF had given undertakings to run food trains, though at first there were considerable problems — as at Milford Haven, where large quantities of fish were without either rail or road transport until the GWR took decisive action. A good assortment of GWR vehicles is visible in this May 12 scene also a van belonging to the Worcester vinegar-makers, Hill Evans & Co., which carries a paper sticker (as do several of the GWR vans and lorries) probably indicating that it is carrying food supplies. The GWR 'Express Cartage Services' lorry on the right is carrying a poster advocating the taking of earlier holidays, with excursions available in May and June, though this sort of traffic would doubtless have been virtually forgotten at this difficult time.

Right: More lady volunteers assisting the GWR during the General Strike, on May 11 1926, as the Topical Press caption described: "Ladies are helping to tend the horses at the Paddington stables on the GWR. Hon. Mrs. Beaumont and Miss Coventry grooming". The very grubby cart (GWR fleet No. 1999) is apparently in need of 'grooming' itself — and note the great height of the very exposed driving seat.

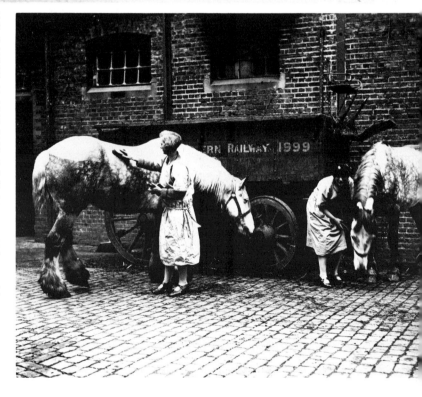

NEWTON ABBOT

NEWTON ABBOT was always one of the most important stations in the West of England: every train to and from Cornwall, and those serving the Torbay resorts, had to pass through, and there was often a great deal of dividing or joining of trains in connection with through carriages to and from the Kingswear Branch. However, the station (which dated from the 1840s) was equipped with only three tracks, serving four platform faces, and a good deal of congestion resulted. A similar situation at Exeter St. David's had been dealt with prior to the First World War, but little was done at Newton Abbot, which remained as a constant 'bottleneck' and a nightmare for the GWR operating department.

At long last, work commenced in 1925, on a radical rebuilding and enlarging at Newton Abbot which resulted in the provision of six running lines, two of these being through 'fast' lines, not served by platforms, while the faces of the two long island platforms were divided into two 'platforms', enabling the station to deal with eight trains simultaneously.

Above: The new station at Newton Abbot was provided with an imposing main building and frontage, seen here shortly after completion and probably prior to the official re-opening, on April 11 1927, which was performed by Lord Mildmay of Flete, a GWR Director and a South Devon 'worthy'. The people of Newton Abbot were very impressed with their station and recorded their appreciation on a plaque which was presented to the GWR to be placed in the entrance hall.

Left: The rebuilding in progress at Newton Abbot seen from the south and showing the erection of the steel girders for the roof over the down platforms, on the right. There is a temporary book stall on the up platform (later Platforms 5 and 6), and a wonderful assortment of platform seats. The hampers on the down platform appear to be for pigeon traffic — for many years an important service rendered to 'the fancy' by all of the 'Big Four' railway companies of the 1923-48 era. Note the workman sitting on the edge of 'up' canopy, surveying the busy scene below.

Right: A view of the modernised station with both the new platform canopies completed, though the up platform has still to be paved at its south end, where a last remnant of the old buildings remain to be demolished. Also surviving from the old station are a pair of the platform gas lamps. Newton Abbot's original station was of the Brunel 'single-sided' type, with the up and down platforms placed end-to-end. The opening of the Torquay branch in December 1848 brought about the provision of a third train shed, quite separate from those for the main line, making three distinct sets of premises! The station was entirely reconstructed in 1861, with three platforms and three running lines under an overall roof: this was the station which had to deal with the ever-increasing volume of traffic, especially at weekends during the holiday period, until the mid-1920s! Adjacent to the station were the Locomotive and Carriage Shops of the South Devon Railway, where the great G.J. Churchward commenced his railway career. These were replaced by new premises in 1894, the site of the old works being used for the erection of a new engine shed — the original one inherited from the South Devon Railway being even more inadequate than was the station.

COLLETT'S 'KING'

Above: Although several GWR 4—4—0s had been fitted with Westinghouse air brake pumps and cylinders for many years, for working stock from other lines, it was not to be expected that No. 6000 would be so equipped, as illustrated here, also in Ranelagh Bridge yard, for GWR main line passenger stock was vacuum braked. The Westinghouse pump was required by the locomotive for working air braked American stock, and as only a very brief period of running-in was allowed between completion and shipping across the Atlantic Ocean, No. 6000 carried the Westinghouse equipment during its trial runs from Paddington. This gave British observers a flavour of 'how things might have been', had British companies adopted air brakes, instead of vacuum brakes, for their rolling stock.

Facing page, lower: It's July 1927, and No. 6000 *King George V* **stands in the Ranelagh Bridge yard, just outside Paddington station, where it was inspected by the GWR's Directors and Chief Officers. An unusual feature of the 'Kings', seen clearly in this view, was the provision of outside frames and springs for the leading bogie wheels, made necessary by the size of the inside cylinders. Some trouble was experienced by the bogie springing, resulting in No. 6003** *King George IV* **being derailed at Midgham — while No. 6000 was en route to America! W.A. Stanier, then Assistant CME at Swindon, who was in charge of the GWR's 'expeditionary force' accompanying No. 6000, received an urgent telegram from Collett forbidding any running by the engine until the modifications had been carried out. Additional coil springs were provided at the sides of the front spring hangers, and the original coil springs on the bogie of No. 6000 were made in America. Collett is supposed to have visited the scene of the derailment, at Midgham, and on poking his umbrella into several sleepers found that the metal tip penetrated the wood. He therefore blamed the Civil Engineer for the derailment, it is said, on the grounds that the track was defective!**

FROM the introduction of Churchward's four-cylinder 'Stars' the GWR could justly claim to have the most efficient express passenger engines in Britain, and with the advent of Collett's 'Castles' the Company laid claim to the most powerful express passenger engine in Britain. However, in 1926 the GWR was 'beaten at its own game' by a most unlikely rival, the Southern Railway. There was no doubt that whilst the Southern's new four-cylinder 4-6-0, No. 850 *Lord Nelson*, had a higher tractive effort (33,500 lbs) than the 'Castle' (31,625 lbs), its efficiency was hardly comparable. Not to be outdone, in the following year the GWR unveiled to the world a locomotive whose tractive effort surpassed that of the 'Castles' by no less than 25%, whilst its adhesive weight of 67 tons 10 cwt easily exceeded that of the Gresley 'Pacifics' of the LNER at 60 tons. Once again, the GWR had produced the undisputed champion!

No. 6000 *King George V* was the result of urgent representations from the dynamic General Manager, Sir Felix J. Pole, for the provision of a much larger and more powerful

Having been 'run in' in the usual manner on local trains from Swindon, No. 6000 *King George V* was put in charge of the 'Cornish Riviera Express' on July 20 1927. The driver and fireman chosen for this auspicious occasion were Young and Pearce, both of Old Oak Common, who were to accompany the engine to the United States. *King George V* stands at the head of the train, at Paddington awaiting the departure time of 10.30am. Described in the contemporary railway press as a 'Super Castle', *King George V* represented the ultimate development of the four-cylinder Churchward 4—6—0. With a tractive effort of 40,300lbs the 'Kings' were the most powerful passenger locomotives in the Kingdom: boiler pressure was 250psi and in true Churchward tradition the barrel was tapered and domeless. The cab was similar in style and facilities to that provided on the 'Castle' and whilst still an improvement on previous GWR practice, its design was still rather austere. The weight of the locomotive and tender in working order was 135 tons 14cwt.

locomotive capable of handling the heaviest trains which could be practically envisaged. The much larger boiler fitted to the new class (the Standard No. 12) had a maximum outside diameter of 6ft, as on the Churchward Standard No. 7 boiler carried by the '4700' class mixed traffic 2-8-0s while the grate area was increased to 34.3 sq ft compared with the 30.28 sq ft of the 'Castles' and '4700s'. Allied to these increases was a record boiler pressure of 250 psi and an increase in both the diameter ($16\frac{1}{4}$ in) and stroke (28 in) of the four cylinders.

The diameter of both the bogie and the driving wheels was reduced compared with the 'Castle' that of the driving wheels being 6ft 6in instead of the standard 6ft 8in and the bogie wheels were 3ft in diameter instead of the hitherto standard 3ft 2in. It has been suggested that the smaller driving wheels were the result of pressure from the General Manager, as the slightly smaller size raised the tractive effort to more than 40,000 lbs, though the real reason was probably that larger wheels would have meant that the engine was slightly over the

maximum height allowed by the loading gauge. The use of smaller bogie wheels was dictated by the need for clearances for the larger cylinders: henceforth all new designs had the smaller-wheeled bogie, though further 'Castles' built from 1932 onwards always had the larger wheels.

Swindon Works had planned to have the new locomotive completed by the end of September, only to be told that it had to be in the United States of America by August! Once again, Sir Felix Pole was responsible. In conversation with a representative of the Baltimore & Ohio Railway, during the 1925 Darlington celebrations, he learnt that the American railway would be celebrating its centenary in 1927 and that the 'B&O' hoped that a representative British locomotive might be present: Pole immediately offered them a GWR example — presumably without the knowledge of either the Directors or Collett! When the new engine was authorised, it was decided that this should be the one to go to the United States; hence the name King George V: the GWR had originally planned to name the class after 'Cathedrals'.

Below: This impressive start from Paddington by *King George V* on the 'Cornish Riviera Express' of July 20 1927 was the prelude to an epoch-making run, for this was the first occasion on which a train of ten carriages was worked unaided from Newton Abbot to Plymouth, over the arduous South Devon banks. After this auspicious start, No. 6000 was exhibited at a number of stations culminating in a triumphant period on display at Swindon, where huge crowds arrived to examine the new 4—6—0. *King George V* looks simply superb in both these photographs; the paintwork carries a deep, beautiful gloss whilst all the exposed copper, brass and steel is burnished to perfection. Driver William Young must have been proud indeed to be in command of Collett's new locomotive. This first run on the down 'Limited' was a triumph, with a gain of five minutes on scheduled time and in his 'British Locomotive Practice and Performance' in the *Railway Magazine*, Cecil J. Allen commented thus: ". . . congratulations are due to Mr. C.B. Collett and his able staff for thus keeping Britain in the forefront of the world's locomotive development."

Right: A head-on view of No. 6000 *King George V* in July 1927, prior to the Baltimore & Ohio Railroad visit, and highlighting the appearance of the Westinghouse air-brake pump. In characteristic style, the GWR's Publicity Department extensively promoted the new locomotive, which was undeniably impressive. On a new series of autumn posters, the 'King' was described thus: "Britain's mightiest to speed you from winter." The speed with which *King George V* was designed and constructed was a fulsome tribute to the ability and capacity of Swindon Works, which produced in the 'King' the most powerful 4—6—0 ever seen in this country.

Below: With the powerful abilities of the new 4—6—0 proved by its brief period of running-in, including the July 20 appearance on the down 'Limited', No. 6000 was prepared for its American visit, and in early August the locomotive arrived at Cardiff Roath Dock, for shipment to Baltimore. On August 4 1927, No. 6000's boiler is prepared for removal from the frames and loading aboard the Bristol City Line's *Chicago City*. Standing behind No. 6000's tender is the *North Star* replica, which accompanied the 'King' to America.

Above: *King George V's* boiler is swung towards the deck of the *Chicago City,* which at only 285ft in length was a relatively modest vessel. In dismantled condition, the 4—6—0 was carried as deck cargo, which must have been quite a challenge for those responsible for stowage. Note the wooden blocks to prevent the chains from the hooks in the firehole damaging the steel backplate and the threaded studs on which boiler fittings were mounted. This picture emphasises the small size of the *Chicago City* whose beam (width) appears roughly comparable with the length of the 'King's' boiler.

Left: Safely on board, *King George V's* boiler rests on a very solidly-built wooden cradle on the deck of the *Chicago City.* The original Topical Press caption described No. 6000 as " the world's fastest engine", doubtless much to the satisfaction of the Company's senior managers and Publicity Department! Note the protective covers over safety valves and chimney, and the deep, glossy finish on the smokebox door.

Right: On arrival in the United States of America, the 'King' was reassembled at the Mount Clare Works of the Baltimore & Ohio Railway. This work was undertaken by the GWR party, which comprised Chargeman Fitter Fred Williams and Leading Hand William Dando, in addition to Driver Young and Fireman Pearce, under the overall supervision of William Stanier. In late November 1927 the process was reversed to enable No. 6000 to return home, and in this picture the chassis is unloaded at Cardiff Docks. Once again, the original, slightly incorrect caption is worth quoting: "Arrival home of 'King George V', the wonderful GSR engine that went too fast for American experts during exhibition tour in America — The great locomotive arrives at Cardiff on the *Chicago Beauty.*" The B&O Company had made facilities available to test the locomotive and train of 543.6 tons (tare) was provided, comprising seven heavy vehicles (average weight — 77.6 tons) including a dynamometer car and two Pullman sleeping cars. Between Baltimore and Washington (38 miles) the maximum speed reached was 74mph, with a maximum drawbar pull of 21,800lbs. On another test run between Washington and Philadelphia (134 miles), the maxima were a speed of 73mph and a drawbar pull of 23,700lbs. The regular GWR crew experienced a few problems with fuel, which was a hard gas coal, and not really suitable for long runs with the type of grate fitted. Clinker formed on the firebars, making it difficult to maintain full boiler pressure — and it must be remembered that neither Driver Young or Fireman Pearce 'knew the road'. Speed was limited to 65mph on this run, on account of curvature and level crossings, but the B&O Company was reported to be both pleased and impressed with the locomotive — especially its smooth working and excellent riding qualities at all speeds.

Above: With the chassis safely back on the rails, No. 6000's boiler is swung onto the dock after its voyage home, in November 1927. The dock workers around the smokebox steady the boiler, whilst colleagues at the rear carefully position a piece of timber to ensure that the ashpan securing studs, which project vertically from the bottom of the firebox foundation ring, are not bent or broken when the boiler is placed on the ground. Whilst in America, No. 6000 was presented with a commemorative bell, which the locomotive (withdrawn in December 1962 and preserved as part of the National Collection) still carries above its leading bufferbeam.

PROMOTING THE GWR

THE majority of advertising by railway companies in the pre-grouping era was aimed at generating increased passenger business, for until the inter-war years the railways enjoyed a virtual monopoly of goods transport, and there was thus little need to promote freight services in earlier years.

Advances in printing at the close of the 19th century, making colour posters available at relatively cheap prices, prompted the rapid development of the railway poster, especially in the period between the turn of the century and the outbreak of the First World War, in 1914. Some posters were humorous, some extolled the healthy environment of the areas being promoted, whilst others made glowing reference to scenery and historic buildings. Many were works of art in their own right and have since become collectors items: facsimile reproductions produced in the last few years have proved popular. There was much competition in the air in these years and maps frequently appeared on the posters, always showing the home company's routes in bold, direct lines, whilst those of competing companies would be circuitous, convoluted and far less prominent generally — or even ignored altogether! This chapter features some classic examples of the poster designer's technique, together with some marvellous hand-drawn examples, produced in chalk on blackboards, by GWR staff.

Left, upper: GWR publicity for the Cornish Riviera area and the prestigious 'Limited' express were always prominent, as illustrated by this group of four particularly attractive examples of the poster designers art. On the top left is a very famous poster, where the GWR rather shamelessly distorted the shape of Cornwall to draw a comparison with Italy, beneath the encouragement to "See your own country first". Said the GWR: "There is a great similarity between Cornwall and Italy in shape, climate and natural beauties."

Left, lower: A fascinating selection of GWR posters advertising an assortment of excursion trains in August-September 1910. A third class excursion ticket from Paddington to Birmingham on Sunday August 13 that year cost five shillings (25p)! On the extreme right, a poster proudly proclaiming 'Important Notice' details 'cheap Saturday to Monday' tickets to selected GWR stations, with minimum first class fares of four shillings (20p) and third class fares of half-a-crown (12½p).

During the 1920s the GWR began to use blackboards to advertise its facilities, and company staff were encouraged to design 'posters' in chalk. In November 1929 a competition was held at Paddington for the best creations, all entries being in the form of photographs of the originals. Some truly amazing efforts were revealed, and as seen on this page, GWR station staff displayed considerable artistic talent.

Right, upper: A group of chalk 'posters' on display at Paddington on November 28 1929 — described by the Topical Press Agency as 'The Power of Chalk!' A British Rail advertising campaign of the mid-1980s which used the slogan "Let the train take the strain" was clearly not original!

Right, lower: More marvellous entries in the chalk 'poster' competition being scrutinised by a GWR company servant, also on November 28 1929.

Left: The winning entry, delicately portraying the West Country, hardly seems possible as a chalk drawing — a tribute indeed to an unknown artist.

GWR ROAD SERVICES

Above: The GWR was a pioneer in the use of bus services to provide feeder services to railheads, and to link towns between which there was no direct line, the first GWR buses entering service between Helston station and The Lizard on August 17 1903. The GWR also started providing sight-seeing tours around London at about the turn of the century, and in 1907, when this photograph was taken, these were operated in conjunction with Motor Jobmasters Ltd, whose buses ran from Paddington station on Tuesdays and Thursdays. Similar tours were also operated from some other London stations. Even then, the American tourist was a source of important business, as indicated by the notice painted beneath the footboards: "SEATS BOOKED at PADDINGTON STATION, car leaves at 10.30am & 2.30pm each TUESDAY & THURSDAY. FARE for ROUND TRIP 4/- (one dollar)." The solid tyred vehicle was chain driven — the guard and chain is visible in front of the rear wheel — and capable of 12mph.

Left: One of the GWR's own vehicles stands at the kerb during a tour of the capital, its canvas top rolled back in the hot weather. Most of the gentlemen are wearing straw 'boaters' and the advertisement above the windows proclaims: 'SPECIAL TRIP to VIEW SIGHTS of LONDON TO & FROM PADDINGTON STATION, GREAT WESTERN RLY.

Right: There was no direct rail link between Oxford and Cheltenham but the towns were connected by the GWR in 1928 by means of a road motor service, using Thorneycroft 15-seat luxury coaches. On October 30 1928, the first day of the new service, eastbound and westbound coaches stop near Northleach to exchange greetings — a practice which would be unthinkable in 'mid section' on any railway! Both buses spent less than two years in GWR ownership, passing to the Western National Company (in which the GWR had a considerable financial interest) in April 1930. The vehicles are YW 5110 (right) and YW 5112, both carrying GWR chocolate and cream livery.

Above: Having safely accomplished its first journey, YW 5112 (GWR Fleet No. 1299) stands under the canopy at Cheltenham St. James Station in readiness for the return run to Oxford Station: The service started from the down approach road and returned to the up approach road, for the convenience of London passengers. Tickets could be purchased at Paddington, thus encouraging through booking: 12/- single (60p) and 15/- return (75p). The normal rail fare, via Gloucester or Kingham was 13/6 single (67½p) and 26/6 return (£1.32½).

Right: The Oxford-Cheltenham service was so popular that larger vehicles were soon required and in March 1929 the Thorneycrofts were replaced by two 25-seat Gilfords, two additional coaches of the same type joining them during the next month. Gilford coach No. UL 9468 (GWR No. 1601) is pictured outside Cheltenham St. James Station.

Above: UL 9468 (GWR No. 1601) passing through Burford. The Gilford coaches had armchair seats, loose cushions, draw curtains and adjustable hot-water heating — the latter in view of the run over the Cotswolds where snow is a regular winter hazard: There were also cigarette, chocolate and match vending machines on board and all the windows could be opened. In the summer of 1929, the service included an extra journey on Sundays from Oxford to Burford and back, competing with the City of Oxford & District Motor Services' route. These vehicles were also painted in chocolate and cream livery.

Above: A superb photograph of a little-known GWR venture, No. 95 was a battery-electric delivery van, built in the Company's Slough workshops in 1906. Propelled by two electric motors and an 80-volt battery, the vehicle had a range of 30 miles on one charge. Braking was by means of callipers on the electric motor shaft, visible in front of the rear wheels. No. 95 could carry a load not exceeding two tons, and among its uses was the carrying of cases of tobacco for W.H. Wills & Co. Side sheets could be unrolled from the van roof to protect the load, but no such facility was available for the driver! In this view, the vehicle is carrying an advertisement for the road motor service between Penzance and Land's End — the service being described as by 'Rail Motor', the term usually given to the GWR's steam railcars and auto-trains.

Below: The early 1930s witnessed a great increase in the number of lorries operated by the GWR, as major developments took place in the company's rail-road goods services. Consequently, 219 new motor lorries and tractors were ordered at a cost of £127,000, 108 of the vehicles being built by Messrs Dennis Bros. at the Guildford works. The first consignment of a dozen 20.36 hp chassis is pictured here ready to leave the works on May 31 1931. The cab sides and nearside windscreen are still unglazed, though a small glass panel has been added to the upper half of the driver's window. Pneumatic tyres have replaced solid tyres, though oil lamps still accompany the electric headlights. The GWR had been one of the first railways to inaugurate country motor lorry services,

the first of which were introduced in the early 1900s in Pembrokeshire (between Llandyssul and New Quay and between Haverfordwest and St. David's) to carry parcels and goods traffic which was too heavy for the roofs of the ordinary railway horse-drawn omnibuses — then the only regular means of transport. Similar facilities were later introduced at Montgomery, St. Clears, Penzance, Helston and St. Austell, with a regular daily service. Whereas in 1925 there had been only eight such services, by the end of 1927 there were no less than 45! Primarily intended to feed traffic on to the railway and to develop business in rural areas, the rates fixed ensured that a small profit was also earned in each area.

Right: Also in 1931, an order was placed with J. Thornycroft & Co., Basingstoke, for 200 chassis, divided equally between 30cwt and 4-ton models. This was the largest order of its kind which had ever been placed with one company at that time. Sixteen of the chassis are pictured ready for delivery, on November 1 1931, the smaller 30cwt vehicles on the left and six of the 4-ton chassis on the right.

Above: A close-up view of one of the Thornycroft 30cwt chassis, built in 1931 at Basingstoke (see also facing page, lower). Note the exposed steering gear in connection with what was then the relatively new feature of 'forward control', also the provision of removable oil lamps, in addition to the two electric headlamps. These lorries were a long-lived breed, and a considerable number were still in use in the late 1940s.

Left: A revolutionary road vehicle introduced during the 1930s was the Scammell 'Mechanical Horse' which replaced the use of real horses in much of the GWR's local cartage work. The transition from horses with four legs to those with three wheels was far from easy, and special driving instruction classes had to be held. These took place at Brentford, Middlesex, where temporary traffic lights and 'Belisha' beacons were installed on a special practice road, as illustrated here on April 20 1936. The intrepid pedestrian, wearing spats and reading a newspaper may have been a salaried staff member of the Goods Department? If so, he was probably a member of the Railway Clerk's Association — which was commonly regarded as 'a cut above' the National Union of Railwaymen, to which the learner driver would have belonged. This vehicle is GWR fleet No. C 2731.

Below: GWR 3-ton Scammell 'Mechanical Horses' No. BGX 600 (Fleet No. C3600) and ALN 361 in use at Brentford, Middlesex, in April 1936, to train former horse cart drivers in the difficult art of reversing an articulated vehicle, whilst a couple of interested colleagues watch from the embankment and bridge in the background. To these railwaymen, the three wheeled Scammells — which are carrying 'L' plates on the cab roofs — must have seemed a real innovation and the original Topical Press caption for this series of photographs was headlined: "Another win for the Machine Age — Railway horses superseded by motor 'horse'." Although of a similar overall design, these two vehicles display a variety of detail differences in both construction and livery. The GWR Express Cartage Services lorry in the background, carrying a peeling advertisement for 'Bisto', is Fleet No. A841; all these vehicles were painted in variations of the traditional chocolate and cream livery.

Right: A consignment of copies of the 'Radio Times' for distribution throughout the West Midlands, South Wales and the West of England, pictured in the hands of the GWR, carried in covered trailer No. T524, and hauled by 3-ton 'Mechanical Horse' No. CGN 978 (GWR Fleet No. C3567). The side doors are open to the elements, but the windscreen at least is glazed — and note the trumpet-type rubber bulb horn protruding through the front panel, above the driver's side of the cab. These 'Mechanical Horses', and subsequent models, became a familiar sight in towns throughout the country, making local deliveries from goods terminals until the early 1960s.

AS might be expected, the Publicity Departments of all railway companies tended to concentrate on their prestige express services, the glamorous 'top link' locomotives, new stations or comfortable new carriages. Drivers retiring from the 'Cornish Riviera Express' after 50 years service found Station Masters, Divisional Superintendents and press photographers awaiting their last arrival at Paddington: on the other hand, the goods link driver would pass quietly and un-noticed into retirement after an equally long period of service for the GWR. Although goods services always provided the foundation of any railway's income, its workaday engines and less glamorous operations rarely attracted any press attention. In the era of loose coupled wagons, wagonload business and intensive freight working, involving much marshalling, remarshalling, empty stock, working and inter-regional traffic, the job of the major yard and the skills of the shunter were especially significant, if largely unseen. His work in coupling and uncoupling wagons, either singly or in 'rafts', and which were frequently moving in several groups at the same time, was fraught with danger. It was his job to divide and remarshall trains smoothly, efficiently and safely, using his nimbleness, skill, brakestick and pole to control the wagons and his lamp to give the shunting locomotive driver signals and instructions. Just as the successful working of a locomotive required teamwork between driver and fireman, so the successful work of a major yard depended on almost telepathic communication, teamwork and skill between driver and shunter. The hard and dangerous work of the shunter rarely received much publicity; however, in 1908 a series of photographs were taken of a shunter at work at

THE GOODS DEPARTMENT

Acton, to the west of London, one of the GWR's largest goods yards. Below: Carrying his brakestick and hand lamp, the shunter emerges from between two open wagons, that on the left being of LNWR ownership, and in rather better condition than the GWR wagon on the right.

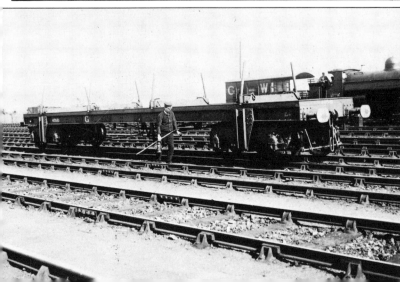

Left: Carrying his pole and lamp in one hand, the shunter trudges along beside GWR bogie bolster wagon No. 40581, which is fitted with large buffers, to prevent buffer locking on sharp curves. Note also the practice of painting the vehicle number on the ends, as well as the sides of the wagon. The 0—6—0ST No. 2779 is one of the '2721' class built at Swindon between 1897 and 1901, at that time the latest and most powerful of the GWR's many classes of 0—6—0ST. Like the majority of the Company's saddle tanks, No. 2779 was later rebuilt as a pannier tank (in February 1928): it was withdrawn in November 1945.

Above: The shunter's brake stick in use, applying the brake of GWR 10-ton wagon No. 3422. The vehicle is in extremely good condition, and the 'O.O Common 15/6/08' chalked on the side door suggests a recent loaded visit to the locomotive shed. The locomotive in the background is one of the 'Metro' class 2—4—0Ts fitted with condensing apparatus, which worked on the GWR's London suburban services for more than 40 years, until the 1920s, when they were displaced by 'Prairie' tanks.

Right, upper: A detailed view of the shunter at work, about to pull the handle free of the ratchet teeth to release the brakes on open wagon No. 3422 (see above). At this time the GWR was flourishing under General Manager J.C. Inglis and statistics reported in the 'Railway Magazine' in 1908, and relating to the 1902-1906 period showed that goods tonnage carried by the GWR had increased from 40,514,061 to 47,174,923, and that the goods wagon fleet had increased from 60,139 vehicles to 66,823. By 1908 the wagon fleet had increased to 68,238 vehicles.

Right, lower: A detailed view illustrating the different type of brake fitted to LNWR coal wagon No. 50220: the brake handle was levered into the 'on' position in precisely the same way as the GWR wagon, but the LNWR brakes were secured by a pin. This was as effective as the ratchet arrangement on GWR wagon No. 3422, but rather slower and more cumbersome in operation. The GWR brakes could be levered into the 'on' position and secured in a single movement with the pole, whereas the 'pin' variety required the brakes to be applied with one hand and 'pinned down' with the other. Shunters frequently 'rode' on their poles as they braked a fast moving single vehicle, or 'raft' of wagons, and anything to make the operation more straightforward — and safer — was doubtless welcomed by the staff involved.

96

Left: The shunter demonstrates how he would walk alongside a moving wagon, brake handle under his control, during marshalling operations. His long hook-ended shunting pole is ready for use: the pole was placed over a buffer shank and the curled hook on the end was used to 'flick' the three link couplings on or off the drawhooks of an adjacent vehicle or locomotive. A skilled practitioner made this procedure appear extremely easy, but it was a technique which demanded much practice and skill to perfect. The hand-lamp would be used to give instructions to the locomotive driver. Note that five-plank wagon No. 20443 is vacuum-brake fitted, and that its number is carried on the end, above the left-hand buffer. This view clearly illustrates the pivot arrangement for the central support, used when the load had to be sheeted over; the tarpaulin would be secured to the small hooks above the bufferbeam.

Above: Much of the GWR's goods business was of a seasonal nature, and this applied especially to agricultural produce, as illustrated in this view of Newton Abbot yard, in October 1908. A variety of horse drawn carts owned by cider makers Henley & Sons are being used to transport apples from the GWR wagons to the cider presses at Abbotskerswell.

Left: Also in the West of England, traffic of a very different kind was provided by the vast quantities of Cornish china clay, much of which was transported over the route of the former Cornwall Minerals Railway (taken over by the GWR in 1877) to the docks at Fowey. In this view, china clay is being loaded into open wagons whilst a mixed goods, probably hauled by a '4500' class 2—6—2T, passes on the line to Newquay.

Right: Out-of-gauge loads always presented special problems, requiring much detailed planning and frequently specialised wagons. On September 2 1934 a 42-ton stator yoke, part of 600 tons of electrical machinery bound for Battersea Power Station, is en route from Paddington to its destination on an LMS 'Weltrol' wagon. The load is pictured passing a signal post at Lots Road, Battersea, with only a few inches to spare. The original caption implies that the track in some locations had to be slewed to create sufficient clearance for the special load.

Below: The original Topical Press caption for this photograph was: "Paddington-on-Sea? Engine drivers and firemen of the GWR Goods Station at Paddington are daily besieged by hungry seagulls who share their lunch. The driver and fireman of a light goods engine feeding seagulls during the lunch hour". The 0—6—0PT, No. 5767, is one of the standard '5700' class, of which no fewer than 863 examples were built between 1929 and 1950. The cab roof appears to have been 'modified' during coaling operations, but the bucket and fire irons on the back of the bunker were standard accessories for the class. This storage position made them difficult to reach, and No. 5767's fireman has propped the 'pricker' behind the tank handrail, adjacent to the cab, to enable easy use without having to stop the engine. Perhaps No. 5767 was not steaming well that day! The horse-drawn cattle wagon on the flat truck must have been a museum piece, even when the photograph was taken, on December 5 1933! Compared with the smaller locomotives used by other railway companies, the GWR's 0—6—0s usually led roving lives. No. 5767 had moved from Southall to Oxford by 1938, while by 1947 it was working from Yeovil and when withdrawn in September 1958 the locomotive was based at Westbury.

Left: Milk traffic by rail was anything but seasonal, being handled daily in vast quantities throughout the year. Until the 1920s, this traffic was transported in thousands of churns carried in covered milk wagons similar in appearance to the well-known cattle trucks, but from 1928 these were increasingly replaced by glass-lined tank wagons. Initially, these were of four-wheeled construction, as illustrated here on December 2 1937, but six-wheeled wagons were also used. Their maintenance was the responsibility of the dairies, who had to wash out the tanks with hot water after each journey. Although special milk trains ran daily from the West of England and South Wales to London, with corresponding 'Returned Milk Empties' workings, several wagons could often be seen attached to the rear of a conveniently-timed passenger train. The tank wagons pictured here are (left-right) No.s 2008, 2009, 2011 and 2007.

THE
CHELTENHAM FLYER
THE WORLD'S FASTEST TRAIN

Above: It's July 9 1923, and the afternoon up 'Cheltenham Spa Express' stands in Swindon station before commencing its first run to Paddington on the new 75-minute schedule, requiring a start-to-stop average speed of 61.8 mph. It might have been expected that one of Churchward's 'Stars' would have been used, but the distinction was given instead to two-cylinder 'Saint' 4—6—0 No. 2915 *Saint Bartholomew*, which made the run in 72 minutes (three minutes inside the schedule) with a load of 300 tons. Built in August 1907, No. 2915 was withdrawn from Chester in October 1950 after working in revenue-earning service for 43 years — and precious few classes originating in the early years of this century could claim such distinction. Note the very ornate lamps on the platform.

IN July 1923, the GWR, which had steadily accelerated its long-distance services, decided to lay claim to the 'blue riband' of railway speed in Great Britain, held until then by the North Eastern Railway (and newly-formed LNER) with its 43-minute run over the 44.1 miles from Darlington to York. The GWR train chosen for this new distinction was the afternoon service from Cheltenham to Paddington, which arrived in London shortly after 5.00pm, but it was only over the almost level and well-aligned stretch from Swindon to Paddington that high speed running was attempted. The timing over the 77.3 miles from Swindon to Paddington was cut to 75 minutes, requiring a start-to-stop average speed of 61.8 mph.

What had been the 'Cheltenham Spa Express' soon became known as the 'Cheltenham Flyer', and although this name never appeared in the time-tables, it was later officially recog-nised through the provision of a distinctive headboard, which also proclaimed that it was the 'fastest train in the world'. This distinction had previously been held by the GWR's Exeter Express during the 1840s and by the 'Flying Dutchman' between 1871 and 1884. However, the headboard was not carried until 1929, when the timing was cut to 70 minutes and the booked speed rose to 66.7 mph. Two years later, in September 1931, after the Canadian Pacific Railway cut the time of its fastest

Left: Also on July 9 1923 at Swindon, No. 2915 *Saint Bartholomew* and its crew, Driver Hopkins and Fireman Bailey, together with a figure seemingly inseparable from any great locomotive occasion on the GWR, Chief Locomotive Inspector George M. Flewellyn, who was on the footplate for the inaugural run of the accelerated schedule — as he had been on the occasion of the 'Record of Records' run by *City of Truro* on May 9 1904, when this famous 4—4—0 was reputed to have been the first locomotive to exceed 100 mph, during an epic descent of Wellington Bank, in Somerset, with a London-bound Ocean Mails special.

Below: *Saint Bartholomew* and its train at Paddington's platform 7 shortly after the conclusion of the record-making run of July 9 1923. The 'Saints' were renowned for their speed, and a Swindon legend credited No. 2903 *Lady of Lyons* with reaching 117 mph as a light engine on trial when running down Dauntsey bank: the future Chief Mechanical Engineer, C.B. Collett, was alleged to have been among those on the footplate on this occasion, though he appears never to have either denied or confirmed this story. The fastest run for several years on this service was by the pioneer four-cylinder engine, No. 4000 *North Star,* which on September 29 1924 did the journey in 71 minutes, following a late start, at an average speed of 65.3 mph.

service from Montreal West to Smith's Falls to 108 minutes for 124 miles (an average speed of 68.9 mph), the GWR again accelerated the 'Cheltenham Flyer' so that the booked time was cut to 67 minutes and the average speed increased again to 69.2 mph. Finally, in September 1932, the time was further reduced, to 65 minutes, thus raising the average speed to 71.4 mph.

The 'Cheltenham Flyer' was still the fastest train in the world and daily carried a headboard to this effect. However, this was mounted on the engine before it left Old Oak Common shed for the outward run to Gloucester on the 10.45am semi-fast service from Paddington and some of the passengers must have pondered that if this was the fastest train in the world,

Right: The first 'Castle' 4—6—0s were running when the accelerations of July 1923 were implemented, but the older 'Star' 4—6—0's still remained in charge of the prestige Cheltenham-Paddington duties, where with loads of around six coaches they were easily masters of their task on the 77.3-miles level road from Swindon. However, in the summer of 1929 the GWR cut a further seven minutes from the Swindon-Paddington schedule, which implied a start-to-stop average of 66.7 mph. Thus, by 1930 'Castles' had replaced the 'Saints' and 'Stars' as normal motive power for the 'Cheltenham Flyer', though the fastest time then recorded had been recorded by a 'Star', which ran from Swindon to Paddington in 66 min. 12 sec. The 'Cheltenham Flyer' is seen here making spectacular progress through the Thames Valley, with a 'Castle' in charge, on October 1 1930.

Above: In 1931, GWR pride was stung when word arrived that on the other side of the Atlantic Ocean, the Canadian Pacific Railway had scheduled its 'Royal York Express', linking Montreal West and Smiths Falls, to run at 68.2 mph westbound and 68.9 mph eastbound — the worlds fastest train! To reclaim the crown the GWR accelerated the 'Cheltenham Flyer' yet again on September 14 1931, when a further 3 minutes were trimmed from the Swindon-Paddington timing, increasing the start-to-stop speed to 69.2 mph, and thus edging in front of the CPR. To ensure that this achievement was appreciated, this acceleration was accompanied by provision of the famous 'World's Fastest Train' headboard for the 'Flyer'. In this scene, No. 5000 *Launceston Castle* is greeted by a group of youngsters as it passes Tilehurst with the inaugural run to the new schedule, on September 14 1931. With Driver Jim Street and Fireman F.W. Sherer in charge, the six-coach load of 190 tons was whisked from Swindon to Paddington in 59 min. 36 sec. start to stop, — an average speed of 77.8 mph, and featuring a maximum speed of 89 mph. Also, apart from a brief spell at 79 mph at Goring (on the water troughs) Jim Street, ably assisted by Sherer's superb firing, kept the speed in excess of 80 mph for no less than 70 miles continuously. On the following day, Driver C. Wasley and Fireman A. Hoyle reduced the overall time to 58½ min, whilst on September 16 Driver H. Jones and Fireman C.E. Brown achieved 58 min. 20 sec. — a world record: *Launceston Castle* was in charge throughout. All three crews were from Old Oak Common, as was Chief Inspector H.J. Robinson, who rode on No. 5000 on all three days. *Launceston Castle*, which had attracted headlines in 1925 when it performed so superbly over the west coast main line during a visit to the LMS, spent more than two decades at Old Oak Common, followed by a spell at Bristol Bath Road before being withdrawn from Oxley Shed, Wolverhampton, in October 1964. The locomotive was then scrapped by Bird's, Swansea, in April 1965.

what were the others like! However, it must be recorded that in 1928 the GWR had 18 trains which ran at an average speed in excess of 58 mph and six of these averaged more than 60 mph.

By 1939, such was the advance in world railway speed, due to the introduction of streamlined diesel-electric trains in Germany and the United States, the 71.4 mph schedule placed the 'Cheltenham Flyer' well below the top 100 of the world's fastest trains. The GWR could not even claim the distinction of running the fastest steam-hauled train, as the 'Cheltenham Flyer' had been beaten by the 71.9 mph of the LNER's 'Coronation' streamliner between London and York. However, unlike the high-speed trains on other rail-

ways, there was no strict limitation of load and the 'Flyer' ran six days a week, with no easing of schedules on Saturdays, even in the height of summer. If the traffic involved extra carriages, then an all-out attempt was made to keep to the advertised time. One carriage over the normal load of seven may not have been a very great challenge, but when the load rose to ten carriages (340 tons full) and No. 5018 *St. Mawes Castle* took only 63 min 04 sec for the 77.3 miles, reaching 82 mph at three places, it was a different matter. Even that achievement was subsequently surpassed, when No. 5023 *Brecon Castle* hauled 13 carriages (435 tons!) from Swindon to Paddington in 71 min 41 sec averaging 76.8 mph over the 42.3 miles from Uffington to Maidenhead!

Below: In 1932 the GWR made its final acceleration to the Swindon-Paddington schedule of the 'Cheltenham Flyer', booking 65 minutes for the 77.3 miles, bringing to British services for the first time a run timed at more than 70 mph — actually 71.4 mph. In the heady spirit of 'being ahead', GWR management and crews rose to the challenge, and just before this new schedule was introduced, a remarkable achievement was recorded. On June 6 1932, a world record run was made by No. 5006 *Tregenna Castle*, with a load of six carriages weighing 186 tons tare, 195 tons full. The time taken for the 77.3 miles was 56 min. 47 sec. and the average speed was 81.6 mph, the maximum speed was 92 mph and 70 miles were covered at an average speed of 87.5 mph. Pictured here are the footplatemen without whom the record run would not have been possible, Driver Ruddock (right) and Fireman Thorpe (left). That this speed record was not a spontaneous effort is evident from the fact that this photograph was taken at Paddington prior to the morning down working!

Left: This picture was taken in September 1932, when the GWR was still determined to secure maximum publicity for its famous train. No. 5016 *Montgomery Castle* is seen at Old Oak Common shed prior to running up to Paddington to work the rather leisurely 10.45am to Gloucester, but already carrying the famous headboard. This had become normal practice, confusing though it must have been for Gloucester-bound patrons, though *Tregenna Castle* had not carried the headboard on the outward working prior to its record run of June 6 1932.

Right, upper: Taken on the same morning as the picture above, the driver and fireman are pictured servicing *Montgomery Castle;* the driver is oiling the outside slide bars, while his mate appears to be checking the tightness of a nut on the motion bracket — doubtless for the benefit of the photographer. The locomotive is beautifully clean, from its Brunswick green paintwork to the cast iron brake blocks! The connecting and side rods have clearly been the result of much effort by the cleaners.

Right, lower: On the footplate of *Montgomery Castle,* with the driver's hand on the regulator handle, and the fireman feeding the glowing fire with another shovel of Welsh steam coal. Like No. 5006, its early years were spent working from Old Oak Common shed, but in 1938 it was the only 'Castle' 4—6—0 based at Penzance (for working the 'Cornish Riviera Express' to and from Plymouth), while its later years were spent in South Wales at Landore (Swansea) and Llanelly. Although rebuilt with a double chimney in February 1961, when it was almost 30 years old, No. 5016 was withdrawn in September of the following year — a sad and telling illustration of the wasteful and badly-planned manner in which steam traction was swept from the network. After withdrawal No. 5016 was stored at Llanelly until the end of November and then scrapped at Cashmore's yard, Newport, in December of that year.

Left: During the 1930s, the photographic press agencies were very fond of depicting large gangs of cleaners at work on locomotives — especially at busy times of the year. This produced interesting 'picture stories' useful to editors when other news was 'thin on the ground'. The original Topical Press caption for this picture, taken on December 12 1933, reads: "The Christmas Clean-up — a mass attack on the famous 'Cheltenham Flyer' engine at Swindon, Wilts, in readiness for the Christmas rush."

Below: By 1937, the GWR could no longer boast that it operated the 'World's Fastest Train' and the famous rectangular headboard disappeared: its replacement, as illustrated on this page, bore more than a passing resemblance to those carried by locomotives working the LNER's named expresses! In this 1937 view, No. 5004 *Llanstephan Castle* leads the 'Cheltenham Flyer' over Goring troughs bound for Paddington. Initially a Laira-based locomotive when new in 1927, No. 5004 soon moved to Paddington, as Old Oak Common was often known, where it spent the greater part of its career. When withdrawn in April 1962 the 4—6—0 was based at Neath: It was scrapped at Swindon works in June of that year.

Above: Among the many experimental innovations of the early years of this century was the introduction of numerous steam railcars — or steam railmotors as the GWR described them — 99 of which were placed in service between 1903 and 1908. Much less well-known was railcar No. 100, pictured here on February 21 1912. This was a petrol-electric vehicle powered by a 40 hp Maudslay petrol engine supplying current to two electric motors mounted on the axle. Sufficient petrol could be carried for a run of 250 miles and the maximum speed was nearly 35 mph. It was designed by the British Thomson-Houston Company, which supplied all the electrical equipment. No. 100 worked on the Windsor branch for several years, but overheating of the detachable valve settings affected the performance of an otherwise entirely effective petrol engine. It was withdrawn in October 1919 and sold to Lever Brothers, Port Sunlight, Cheshire, who used it to carry passengers over their private railway. It was dismantled circa 1923, the body being sold to a member of their staff, who converted it into an attractive summer bungalow at Gronant Beach, near Prestatyn, where it may still exist. Note the roof-mounted radiator!

PASSENGER COMFORT

Right: Although No. 100's petrol-electric propulsion provided a smoother ride than that on a steam railcar or auto-train, little appears to have been done to provide comfortable seating. This interior view of the 44-seat railcar, also on February 21 1912, suggests that it was comparable with that of the average steam railcar of that period. The reversible seating was a feature of the GWR's 'steam railmotors' and auto-trains, and many electric tramway vehicles.

Top: The clerestory roof was a feature of GWR carriages built between circa 1876 and 1904, though it was first used as early as 1838 on the GWR in the 'posting carriages' (an early form of saloon carriage), while the traditional low or flat-roofed design continued to be built, especially for branch and suburban services, until the turn of the century. This vehicle, No. 8314, was one of six 58ft corridor first class carriages built between 1902 and 1904; one of the last clerestory designs built for main line use. No. 8314 is seen here at Fishguard Harbour station on August 30 1909, when it was the final vehicle on one of the two *Mauretania* specials carrying trans-Atlantic passengers to Paddington.

Above: Prior to 1928, the convenience and comfort of the sleeping car could only be enjoyed by first class passengers. However, in September 1928, in common with the LMS and the LNER, the GWR introduced its first third class sleeping cars. The three carriages (Nos. 5140-42) contained five ordinary compartments in addition to three sleeping compartments to provide a total of 12 beds — the lower bunks being of the couchette type. These carriages were introduced on the overnight service between Paddington and Neyland in West Wales. Two of these carriages were later converted to provide eight sleeping compartments apiece, while the third was rebuilt as a composite first class and third class sleeping car (No. 9079). Pictured here on September 19 1928 is car No. 5140.

Left: An interior view of one of the third class sleeping compartments of 1928. The small steps provided to facilitate access to the upper bunk carry the vehicle number (5140) — and note splendid 'Poirot' moustache on the 'slumbering' gentleman in the lower bunk!

Right: This picture, produced on January 23 1932, is best described by its original Topical Press caption: "Automatic Chocolate Boys' on Great Western Expresses. An additional convenience for the travelling public is to be provided by the GWR which is to instal automatic chocolate machines in the corridors of 16 of its principal main line expresses, including both the 'up' and 'down' Cornish Riviera and Torbay Expresses. On the front of the machine is fitted a mirror. A fair traveller making use of the chocolate machine installed today, on the Paddington to Weston-super-Mare express." The machine delivered 'Caley's Marching Chocolate' (full weight) at 1d per bar and to ensure value for money, an inscription on the machine reads: "Look inside wrapper for novel puzzle and particulars of gift scheme."

Left: More substantial fare was provided on a number of short-distance express trains by means of buffet cars. The first examples of these new catering cars were adapted from much older stock, as in the case of this clerestory vehicle, with its superb panelled ceiling and walls, which was used on the Paddington and Oxford service. Gas lighting was still used when this photograph was taken, on July 6 1932.

Right: Much more modern styling and accommodation was provided in those buffet cars built specially for the purpose. This vehicle, complete with sprigs of mistletoe hanging from the ceiling (not a standard feature!) ran on the Paddington and Bristol service in 1934, prior to the introduction of the 'The Bristolian' which commemorated the GWR's Centenary, in 1935. That the mistletoe was not simply for decoration but served a practical purpose is clearly shown in this photograph. This photograph was taken on December 29 1934 — the 'Sixth Day of Christmas' — so the Company evidently kept the festive celebrations going until Twelfth Night!

Right: F.W. Hawksworth became Chief Mechanical Engineer and assumed command of the GWR's locomotives and rolling stock in 1941, following the retirement of C.B. Collett. Despite the restrictions of war-time conditions, design work was undertaken on an entirely new range of carriages, the first examples entering service late in 1946. Externally there was a marked difference from the pre-war designs, the most notable feature being the use of an elliptical roof similar to that used on the LNER. Internally also there was also a 'new look', with considerable use of light-coloured wood veneers, while a new design of metal grille luggage rack was introduced. Seen here is the interior of a third class compartment. These were widely commended as being the most comfortable third class carriages ever to have been provided on any railway in Britain. However, in contrast to the LMS and LNER the GWR still insisted that third class passengers should be expected to sit four aside.

Left: The post-war return to more normal railway operation included a gradual reintroduction of restaurant car services, which had been withdrawn for the duration of the war. Seen here is the interior of the new Hawksworth first class dining car, the seating being arranged to provide tables for two persons on one side and four persons on the other side of the offset gangway. The seats were similar to those used in the 'Centenary Stock' first class dining cars in 1935, and resembled swivelling office chairs!

Below: Passenger comfort of a very different and revolutionary kind was introduced on April 12 1933, when a GWR air service commenced between Plymouth, Torquay and Cardiff, and this was extended to serve Birmingham just over a month later, on May 15. Torquay, Teignmouth and Exeter passengers used Haldon Aerodrome and there was a daily flight in each direction, including Sundays. Initially, six-seater aircraft of this Westland 'Wessex' type, having three engines, were employed, which together with their crews, were provided by Imperial Airways, whose name appeared beneath that of the Great Western Railway on the fuselage. This particular aircraft was painted in chocolate and cream livery, with the Company crest on the trail. The first public air service, linking Hounslow and Paris, had started in 1919, and during the 1920s each of the 'Big Four' companies came to appreciate the commercial threat posed by air travel, and the GWR, LMS, LNER and SR each promoted an Air Transport Bill in 1929, the Royal Assent being granted on May 10 that year. Early in 1934 the 'Big Four' companies, in association with Imperial Airways, formed Railway Air Services Ltd., with a capital of £50,000. The GWR air service was taken over and extended to link Plymouth and Liverpool; De Havilland Dragon Rapide aircraft were subsequently used. Under the hand of the GWR's K.W.C. Grand, later General Manager of British Railways (Western Region), RAS made much progress — from August 20 1934 its aircraft carried the mails.

Above: Although not providing as much room and comfort as the first class dining cars, the Hawksworth third class dining carriages were quite superb for their time. As illustrated here, there was again an extensive use of light-coloured wood veneers, not to mention what has been rather rudely described as the 'Mickey Mouse' style of clock face!

COMPANY SERVANTS

Above: Churchward 'Star' 4—6—0 No. 4041 *Prince of Wales* with its driver and fireman, accompanied by the legendary and redoubtable George M. Flewellyn, Chief Locomotive Inspector. His railway career began as a cleaner at Bristol shed in April 1878, at the age of 16. He became a pilot fireman after six years, and passed as a driver in January 1893. Promoted to main line driver at Plymouth in April 1897, he received rapid promotion to Inspector at Newton Abbot in June 1901 — evidence of his outstanding ability. He was on the footplate of *City of Truro* on the occasion of the 'Record of Records' run in May 1904, when that engine is claimed to have attained a speed of more than 100 mph on Wellington bank. His final position was as Chief Locomotive Inspector at Swindon, during which time he was on the footplate during the inaugural run of the 'Cheltenham Flyer' on July 9 1923, and his career culminated in being one of the footplate party when No. 4082 *Windsor Castle* was driven by His Royal Highness King George V, on the occasion of the Royal Visit to Swindon Works in April 1924. This picture was taken at Paddington in June 1922, following a royal train working in connection with the homecoming of HRH The Prince of Wales (the future Edward VIII) from his Indian tour, which had also included visits to Egypt and Gibraltar. He landed at Plymouth on June 21 1922 and was conveyed to London by the GWR, under the guidance of Chief Inspector Flewellyn. Arrival at Paddington was at 3.30pm, where the train was met by HRH King George V, HRH Queen Mary, and HRH Queen Alexandra.

Left: On June 18 1929, Chief Ticket Inspector Ward presents a distinguished figure at Paddington, alongside a splendid example of a third class clerestory carriage. Chief Inspector Ward had joined the GWR as a ticket examiner at Paddington in November 1883 and was due to retire in July 1929, after 45 years service. The GWR coat-of-arms on the carriageside comprised the arms of the cities of London and Bristol, the linking of which by rail was the origin of the GWR. Used initially with an oval-shaped garter, in the style common to many other company arms, the garter was subsequently discarded.

Right: The photographer attracts the attention of passengers at Paddington as guard Purdie prepares to despatch the 'Cornish Riviera Express' on his last day of service before retirement, in June 1926. In the later 1920s, the 'limited' usually comprised 14 coaches of 498 tons tare, producing a loaded weight of 530 tons.

Above, left: A jolly scene at Paddington in June 1931 as colleagues bid a hearty 'farewell' to travelling ticket collector Charles Hill (third right) on the day of his retirement. The gentleman on the left, wearing wing collar and black bow tie, was a train steward, as indicated by the 'Restaurant Car' badge embroidered into his lapels.

Above, right: The fierce pride in the job, particularly characteristic of uniformed railwaymen of this era, is powerfully conveyed by this portrait of Chief Inspector Thorsey, on the occasion of his retirement, in October 1930. In service with the company for no less than 53 years, Chief Inspector Thorsey was in charge of the GWR royal train for 20 years — distinguished service indeed.

Left: Station gardens were often a great credit to the local staff, who devoted considerable time and energy in creating a display which would both impress the public and overshadow the gardens at other stations! A fine example, with a sub-tropical atmosphere, is pictured here in 1926 at Totnes, which won the GWR 'Best Kept Station' cup that year. The branch to Ashburton closed on November 3 1958 and whilst plans by preservationists to save the whole branch failed (as a result of road improvements, the Buckfastleigh-Ashburton section was lost) the Buckfastleigh-Totnes (Riverside) section was reopened on April 5 1969, by the Dart Valley Railway Company.

Above: In 1937 the Company offered prizes totalling £500 in an 'all line' competition for the best station garden in each of the 12 Divisions. The staff at Pangbourne are pictured here in June of that year, planting the flower beds in readiness for the forthcoming competition. It is just as well that the approaching express behind its 'King' is on the through line, as the attitude of the staff is obviously: "Bother the trains, let's get on with the gardening"!

Right: The press agencies were very fond of staging pictures where an array of locomotives were being worked upon by a small army of cleaners. Taken on December 12 1933, this view purports to show GWR locomotive staff at Swindon preparing locomotives for the 'Christmas rush'. The picture shows three 'King' 4—6—0s and a 'Castle' 4—6—0 (on the right): the 'King' on the left is one of the 1927-28 Lot, the other two being from the second Lot built in 1930, the distinguishing feature being the valve covers for the inside cylinders.

Left, upper: The GWR was always very keen on what were originally known as 'Staff Improvement Classes', through which staff in all Departments were encouraged to improve their knowledge of railway working and improve their efficiency. About 10,000 employees — around 10% of the total staff — took advantage of these classes each year. The original Topical Press Agency caption to this October 9 1935 photograph reads: "A Great Western Railway electrician showing some of his pupils the working of a main line signal with a full size model at a class at Paddington station." A variety of other 'S&T' equipment is also available for demonstration including a single line tablet machine (extreme left) and a selection of block instruments and bells (on the shelf in the background).

Left, lower: A very impressive model railway layout, with fully interlocked miniature signals and levers was also used for instructional purposes at Paddington. A demonstration is in progress here by the same instructor, and involving one of the same students, as the picture above. The signal in the picture above is visible in the left background — this room must have been truly fascinating!

Left: During 1930 the GWR ordered 136,000 experimental steel sleepers, sufficient to cover the equivalent of 60 miles of track. Among the sections on which the rails were relaid with the new sleepers was a stretch, just over a mile long, on the main line near Maidenhead, seen here with the discarded wooden sleepers alongside the new track on August 26 1930. By this time, 60,000 steel sleepers had been laid and the GWR anticipated installing the remaining 76,000 by the year-end.

Right: A close-up view of the pressed steel sleepers being laid at Maidenhead: both pictures on this page emphasise the highly labour-intensive nature of manual permanent way work, with 24 men required to place a single rail in its chairs.

PADDINGTON MODERNISATION

ALTHOUGH Paddington station had been enlarged by the provision of three additional arrival platforms under a new roof span between 1913 and 1915, all the platforms (apart from Nos. 1—3 on the departure side) were quite short by modern standards. All trains, whether main line or suburban, had to depart by means of one down running line, ensuring that one of the worst 'bottlenecks' on the entire GWR system was immediately outside its London terminus. Furthermore, the area between the buffer stops and the Great Western Royal Hotel, always known as 'the Lawn' was used for parcel traffic, leaving little space for passengers to circulate around the platform ends, and the greatly increased number of parcels could not be handled without considerable difficulty. There was thus more than enough justification for radical improvement in the layout and amenities of the GWR's premier station.

Effecting improvements not only involved the Company in very considerable capital expenditure, but also caused numerous problems in operating the train service during the period of modernisation. The approach lines were completely remodelled to permit the lengthening of all the platforms (with the exception of the famous No. 1 Platform, from which all prestige trains departed) and to allow a considerable amount of parallel working of engines and stock. What had been known as Bishop's Road station was completely rebuilt

Above: On August 24 1930, excavations begin at Paddington for the complete rebuilding of the old Bishop's Road Station. The tunnel of the Metropolitan Railway was situated in the foreground of this photograph, and it can be seen that the canal was uncomfortably close to its path! Bishop's Road station was the point at which the GWR made an end-on connection with the Metropolitan Railway, which surfaced at this point. Paddington's main platforms were to the left of this scene, and parallel to the canal: In the course of this modernisation the terminus expanded sideways to occupy this location. On completion of the work, this area formed the suburban side of the terminus (platforms 13-16) and Bishop's Road Station ceased to exist as a separate facility from Monday September 11 1933.

Right: The approach lines to platforms 7 (right) and 8 (left) on June 21 1931, the former having already been lengthened. The familiar covered way on the left would soon be swept away and replaced by an extension of the footbridge which already linked platforms 1-8. On the right, an 0—6—0PT enters the station, probably with empty carriage stock for No. 5 platform, while a 'Castle' stands at the head of a train about to depart from No. 3 platform. The construction of powerful locomotives capable of hauling trains of increasing weight had prompted the need for longer platforms, and this modernisation programme provided three platforms of more than 1,150ft, one of 1,090ft and four of more than 940ft in length. When complete, the parts of the platforms projecting beyond the main roof were provided with canopies. To streamline train working into the new and extended platforms, the main line approaches were remodelled over a ¾-mile distance, and the Ranelagh Bridge locomotive yard facilities were also improved.

Left: On June 21 1931, a 'Castle' 4—6—0 on an up train approaches No. 9 platform, yet to be lengthened at this time, while work continues with relaying the track-work to allow for the extension of the arrival platforms. Either a 'Metro' class 2—4—0T or a '633' class 0—6—0 side tank is in charge of the crane.

Right: Much of the lifting of the track and materials required for the modernisation was done by one of the GWR's three 0—6—4 crane tanks, normally to be found either at Swindon Works or at the northern works at Stafford Road, Wolverhampton. Pictured here is No. 16 *Hercules*, which was built at Swindon in 1921 and very similar in design to 0—6—4CTs Nos. 17 *Cyclops* and 18 *Steropes*, built at Swindon in April 1901. Nos. 17 and 18 were broadly similar to the Wolverhampton-built small 0—6—0Ts of the 850 class, but were fitted with domeless boilers to allow the crane jib to be lowered parallel to the boiler, and extended frames, to carry the crane, under which was a bogie. They were amongst the first GWR locomotives to be fitted with pannier tanks. On June 21 1931, *Hercules* is being used for positioning new platform edging. The crane had a lifting capacity of 6 tons at 18ft jib radius and 9 tons at 12ft. This was among the last work done by this engine, which was withdrawn together with *Cyclops* and *Steropes* in September 1936. The improvements in handling facilities, not least at Swindon Works, had made these fascinating locomotives redundant.

and incorporated fully into the main station.

Bishop's Road was concerned only with trains to and from the Metropolitan Railway, some of which worked between GWR suburban stations and the City, changing over from steam to electric traction at Bishop's Road. It was decided that the station was to be completely rebuilt to provide a terminal point for GWR suburban traffic together with through platforms for trains to and from the Metropolitan line. This involved engineering works of considerable magnitude as part of the old tunnel leading to the Metropolitan system had to be demolished for part of its

length, to provide the required width for four platform roads. New goods and cab approaches had to be built and the enlarged entrance was built in the form of a covered way. What was then the heaviest plate girder in Great Britain, having a length of 133ft and weighing 126 tons, had to be installed to support an area of no less than 4,502 sq ft of the goods and cab approaches, thus allowing a clear space underneath for the new station. At the conclusion of this work, Bishop's Road station ceased to exist as an independent facility, the new layout becoming Platforms 13-16 of Paddington station.

The parcels traffic removed from

'The Lawn' was relocated on what had been the old 'A' excursion platform, an extension of the famous No. 1 platform stretching to beyond Westbourne Bridge — and traditionally used as an observation point by railway enthusiasts and for photographing departing trains. The enthusiasts and photographers were henceforth excluded, but the public gained a spacious circulating area on 'The Lawn' which is still enjoyed today. The opening-up of the area was accompanied by the provision of modern office buildings and refreshment rooms, the latter replacing some most inadequate premises off No. 1 platform.

Right: Whilst it might be difficult to believe, this is actually the famous 'Lawn' at Paddington, during rebuilding on February 14 1933. The parcels traffic which formerly congested it having been banished to the outer darkness of Platform 'A', work is under way on the provision of the new refreshment rooms (bottom right) and the new offices. The exposed ironwork grille ends of the train sheds can be seen to great advantage. The work pictured here transformed the 'Lawn' into a spacious circulating area, roofed in steel and glass and served directly by refreshment, seat registration and lost property facilities. The train indicator, formerly located between platforms 8 and 9, was also moved to this area, from which access was provided to the London Underground. This modernisation scheme was completed during 1934.

Above: Also included in the modernisation programme for Paddington was the replacement of the semaphore signalling by colour lights. Although the LMS and the Southern Railway had installed three and four-aspect signals, and three aspect signals were in course of construction on the LNER, there being in existence general agreement that there should be a complete break with traditional semaphore practice, the GWR did not concur with the other three companies on the best method to adopt. The existing principles of manual block, with the special GWR refinements, coupled with the unique Automatic Train Control (ATC), were considered to be safer. So, the GWR's new signals were unique, as the colour lights displayed precisely the basic signal indications that would have been seen from semaphore signals at night. Both 'stop' and 'distant' signals were retained, the former displaying red or green, and the latter green or amber. The new signals were of the so-called searchlight type, and in some instances two units were mounted on a single mast to provide the indications of the traditional semaphore combined 'home and distant' assembly. This photograph, taken in 1934, shows the new colour light signals on the approaches to Paddington: the system was eventually extended as far west as Southall. 'Hall' class No. 5940 *Whitbourne Hall* built in August 1933, of Stafford Road shed, is approaching the rear of a gantry on which are mounted five of the colour light signals for the main line, with a shunting signal on the right. Note the ATC ramp beneath the gantry. A mixed selection of Churchward, Collett and Dean (clerestory) carriages on the right includes a Churchward 'Toplight' vehicle, newly outshopped with a white roof. No. 5940 was withdrawn from Bristol St. Philips Marsh shed in September 1962.

THE GWR ON FILM

OCCASIONALLY, through an old newsreel, or in a vintage feature film, we can catch a fleeting glimpse of the GWR in the 1920s and 1930s, and the pictures on this page give an indication of how such fascinating pieces of film were produced.

Left: The original Topical Press caption for this photograph reads: "The 'Cornish Riviera' Express was taken to a branch line yesterday to play an important part in the new English talkie 'The Ghost Train'. The filming was done at Bramley, near Basingstoke. Photo shows: Director and cameraman being run down alongside the 'Cornish Riviera' Express. 1st June 1931." This was indulging in a little 'journalists licence', for while the carriages may have carried 'Cornish Riviera Express' destination boards, 'Castles' were not normally used on that prestige working after the introduction of the 'Kings' in 1927. However, No. 5006 *Tregenna Castle* achieved fame in a more lasting manner just over a year later, on June 6 1932, when it made a world record run on the 'Cheltenham Flyer' at an average speed of 81.6 mph.

Right, upper: Less romantic, but more factual, was the Sound News film made in the same year featuring the GWR's Automatic Train Control system. This originated in 1906 when experiments were carried out on the Henley-on-Thames Branch. The electric ramp between the rails gave an audible warning of a distant signal, in the cab of an engine passing over it, and was based on the 'fail safe' system. The ramp raised a plunger on the engine and this sounded a vacuum-siren in the cab and also applied the vacuum brakes. If the signal was 'off', current was applied to the ramp and collected on the engine to counteract the opening of the vacuum valve and ringing an 'all clear' bell instead. The film was made in the Slough area, and the caption records: "The special train, upon which the cinematrographer was operating, was travelling at 82 mph". On March 16 1931, the Torquay and Paignton train, hauled by a 'King', has a fine example of a Churchward 'Concertina' as its first vehicle, while the special train for the film crew is hauled by a 'Castle'. The car on the flat truck is being used as a sound recording studio!

Right, lower: The special filming train at Slough station, also on March 16 1931, showing how the camera was mounted on the tender: the thought of travelling in such a position at a speed of 82 mph (as illustrated above) is rather daunting! The up train is hauled by one of Churchward's 'Saint' class 4—6—0s.

DESPITE being the most safety-conscious of all railways, even the GWR suffered an occasional accident. However, these were generally far less spectacular than those which happened on other lines, nor was there such a dreadful toll of deaths and injuries. The gradual extension of the well-tried ATC (Automatic Train Control) system to cover all the main lines was undoubtedly a major factor in the creation of the GWR's enviable record in respect of safety. However, 'even Jove nods' — especially in places where the ATC system was not applicable.

The Grouping was still in the future when, on January 26, 1921, the

MISHAPS

Cambrian Railways main line was the scene of a horrific head-on collision at Abermule, between Montgomery and Newtown, on a single line section. The trains involved were the 10.05am 'stopping' train from Whitchurch and the Aberystwyth-Manchester express. Both engines were damaged beyond repair while the leading carriages of the express were telescoped and wrecked, 15 persons being killed, including Lord Herbert Vane-

Tempest, a Director of the Cambrian Railways.

Also travelling on the express was Mr. George, the Cambrian Railways Chief Traffic Inspector, who discovered that due to a lamentable series of human errors the crew of the stopping train, (both killed) had wrongly been carrying the Abermule — Montgomery tablet and not that for the Abermule -Newton section. Miraculously, Driver Pritchard Jones and Fireman Owen on the express engine escaped death, though the boiler of their engine was torn out of the frames and twisted through 180 degrees! This terrible mishap is illustrated in this section.

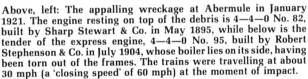

Above, left: The appalling wreckage at Abermule in January 1921. The engine resting on top of the debris is 4—4—0 No. 82, built by Sharp Stewart & Co. in May 1895, while below is the tender of the express engine, 4—4—0 No. 95, built by Robert Stephenson & Co. in July 1904, whose boiler lies on its side, having been torn out of the frames. The trains were travelling at about 30 mph (a 'closing speed' of 60 mph) at the moment of impact.

Above, right: The telescoped front carriages of the express at Abermule, mostly of LNWR stock, though the Pwllheli and Shrewsbury carriage, which incredibly escaped destruction, is a Cambrian Railways' vehicle. It was several days before the line could be opened for traffic.

Right: Less serious was the derailment of this engine — possibly a 'Bulldog' 4—4—0 — at Plymouth Millbay in 1924. It appears to have run off the short facing spur from a catch point and plunged down the embankment from Harwell Street. The driver and fireman were overwhelmed by an avalanche of coal from the tender, and had a narrow escape from death. The use of the LMS tarpaulins to cover the victim suggests that the GWR were trying to convince the public that "it isn't one of our engines!"

Right: This picture clearly illustrates how fatalities and terrible injuries resulted from collisions where 'telescoping' of carriages occurred. In this incident, auto-trailer No. 137 ran into a line of carriages at Old Oak Common in 1927. A suburban 74ft vehicle with 63 seats, this was originally steam railmotor No. 47, built in February 1905 and converted as an auto-trailer in October 1922. A 'County' class 4—4—0 stands beyond the wrecked clerestory carriage, the non-damaged stock having been removed.

Below: Ten years later, and auto-trailer No. 211 has suffered a similar accident on November 16 1937, but this time the collision has been with a stop block and signal box. Dense fog which blanketed parts of London was the cause of the accident at Ealing Broadway station, when the auto-train leaving for Denham ran along a dead-end line, crashed into the stop block and collided with the signal box. The locomotive would have been propelling the auto-trailer. Originally steam railmotor No. 81, No. 211 was a 68ft 6in vehicle seating 45 passengers and intended for use on branch lines; it had only been converted as an auto-trailer two years prior to the accident.

Left, lower: By far the worst accident on the GWR during the inter-war years happened at Shrivenham on January 15 1936. An Aberdare-Old Oak Common coal train, consisting of 53 wooden-bodied wagons hauled by 2—8—0 No. 2801 was accepted by the Shrivenham signalman, who passed it through safely — as he thought. However, the line was obscured by smoke from the 1.50am Kensington-Chippenham milk empties, which was running an hour late, and he failed to check the tail lamp of the coal train. A few minutes later, the 8.40pm sleeping car train from Penzance was accepted, it being assumed that the coal train was safely 'out of section'. Unfortunately, the coal train had divided, due to intense cold acting on an internally flawed metal coupling, and five wagons and the guards van had come to rest on the main line — only 131 yards short of the security of the Shrivenham 'approach track circuit': the guard thought that they had stopped at Shrivenham up home signal. Travelling at between 50 and 60 mph No. 6007 *King William III*, with Driver Starr and Fireman Cozens, both 'top link' Newton Abbot enginemen, struck the van, rode over the top of the goods wagons and guards van, and rolled over. The guard of the coal train had dived out of his van when he saw the 'King' approaching, and was uninjured. The first indication the signalman had of the accident was the sound of the impact and the sight of two coal wagons 'shooting past' the signal box! Driver Starr and one passenger were killed, and ten passengers were seriously injured. In this view, No. 6007 *King William III* lies on its side, smokebox door gaping open and its chimney sitting on the embankment. No. 6007 was withdrawn as a result of this accident, and was replaced at a cost of £5,362. Although officially a new engine, No. 6007 was actually a true 'renewal' as the damage was not beyond repair: this is evident from the cost of the 'new' engine, compared with the cost in 1927 of the 'old' No. 6007, which was £6,383.

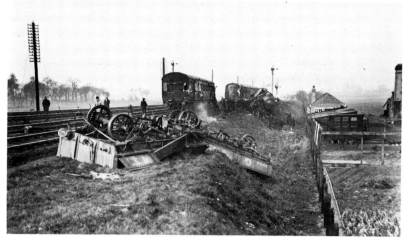

Right, above: The original Topical Press caption for this March 2 1937 picture is: "A guard was killed and six other persons injured when an Oxford to Paddington train collided with a goods train outside Langley (Bucks) station last night." In this general view of the mishap, the engine, a Churchward Mogul; is still carrying a headlamp at the top of the smokebox, which suggests that it was heading a class 'F' Through Fast Goods and not a ballast train — despite all the wagons visible being low-sided permanent-way vehicles. This is the sort of press coverage the publicity-conscious GWR would have happily forgone.

Right, lower: A view of the '4300' class 2—6—0 seen from an unusual angle, having come to rest on the slope of the embankment: it is clear how perilously close the locomotive came to rolling completely over, which would have made the task of recovery considerably more difficult for the breakdown gang.

Below: This dramatic head-on collision occurred at the Dolphin Junction diamond crossing, near Slough, in 1941 when Stanier '8F' 2—8—0 No. 8293 ran through adverse signals in the early hours of the morning and struck the up night service from Plymouth to Paddington, hauled by a 'Castle' 4—6—0. By the time this picture was taken, the 'Castle's' train has been removed and a steam crane is at work, clearing wreckage. No. 8293 was one of 25 '8F' 2—8—0s loaned to the GWR by the LMS in 1940, to alleviate a traction shortage, and this accident was attributed to the 2—8—0 not being fitted with ATC equipment. No. 8293 was the last of the 25 loaned locomotives to be returned to the LMS, in October 1941 — probably after a visit to Swindon for repairs!

RETURN TO SWINDON WORKS

ROYALTY were not the only visitors to Swindon Works, and on February 24, 1927 a party of 100 Eton Collegers paid a visit 'for practical mechanical and engineering instruction in railway construction'. Remembering how the Provost of Eton had protested vigorously against the advent of the GWR in 1835 — "No public good whatever could possibly come from such an undertaking, and he should be wanting in his duty to the establishment over which he presided if he did not oppose it to the utmost of his ability" — one wonders what he would have thought!

Left: During the visit to Swindon Works by Eton scholars, on February 24 1927, 'Star' class 4—6—0 No. 4019 *Knight Templar* is viewed from below as it is lifted by one of the travelling cranes: the bogie centre-pin bearing can be seen quite clearly. No. 4019 was one of a number of 'Stars' later rebuilt with outside steam pipes: this work was done in May 1948 and No. 4019 was withdrawn in October 1949! On the left is steam railmotor No. 65, which was one of the last two examples to remain in service: with No. 70, it worked the last steam railcar service, between Neath and Court Sart, in October 1935. A steam railmotor vertical boiler can be seen below the coupled wheels of the suspended 'Star'.

Right: In May 1929 a party of French Railway Officials visited both Swindon Works and the GWR Docks at Cardiff. They are seen here watching the wheel balancing machine, which carried driving wheels on sprung centres (visible on the left). Lead was added to the balance weights until oscillation at high speed — as in this view — was minimised. Note the brakes to quickly stop the wheels, either to enable the addition of more lead, or when the balancing task was completed. Note also the complete absence of protective guards, making this a highly dangerous piece of equipment.

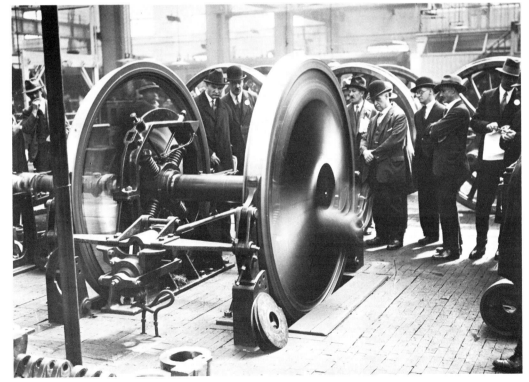

Right: A spectacle of sound and vision which must have been awesome to witness first-hand: 'Castle' No. 4009 *Shooting Star* running at high speed on the works test plant on January 26 1932. The magnificent new 'A' shop, planned by G.J. Churchward as the centre-piece of the modernisation of Swindon Works, included a testing plant for 'running in' locomotives when new, or after a heavy repair. The rollers were driven by compressed air. However, the idea was not very successful, as the plant could not reproduce the external stresses on the wheels and frames transmitted from the conditions and curvature of the track. The original plans for the foundations of the 'A' shop reveal that it was intended that there should be four of these plants! However, little use was made of what was popularly known as the "home trainer" until it was considerably enlarged and modernised under the direction of C.B. Collett. Considerable insularity, amounting to virtual secrecy, marked Swindon during Collett's time, so that the modernisation of the test plant was generally unknown outside GWR circles. When Gresley (of the LNER) and Stanier (of the LMS) became interested in the possibilities of constructing a national test centre, approaches were made to Collett to enlist his possible support; however, he simply took the delegation into the test plant where they were confronted by the spectacle of a 'King' going 'all out' on the vastly improved Swindon installation! *Shooting Star* was one of the half-dozen 'Stars' rebuilt as 'Castles' during the 1920s. (See also rear jacket).

Below: Two 'Kings', Nos. 6007 *King William III* (left) and 6018 *King Henry VI* stand in the erecting shop, on April 20 1932. No. 6007 was fated to be withdrawn in 1936, following the Shrivenham Disaster, and replaced by a 'new' No. 6007, while No. 6018 was widely considered to be the finest member of the class, hence its selection to represent the GWR in the Inter-Regional Trials, in 1948. No. 6007 spent much of its life (or lives!) working from Old Oak Common, apart from a few months in 1936 and 1959 spent at Laira, though for its last three years it was shedded at Wolverhampton, Stafford Road. In contrast, No. 6018 was usually shedded in the West of England, 19 years being spent at Newton Abbot, but it also spent short periods working from Old Oak Common and Bristol Bath Road, while its final shed at Cardiff Canton. No. 6007 was withdrawn in September 1962 and No. 6018 in the following December. The relative positions of the outside and inside cylinders in the classic GWR four-cylinder 4—6—0 type can clearly be seen. On the right is 'County tank' No. 2235: this was probably the last heavy repair for that engine, withdrawn in 1935.

Left: A closer look at No. 6007 *King William III*, also on April 20 1932, undergoing the attention of the Swindon Works fitters and boilersmiths. Note the cleverly counter-balanced hand rivetting machine being used on the firebox. With a grate area of 34.3 sq ft and a length of 11ft 6in these were the longest and largest fireboxes of any GWR standard engines — even the famous 'Pacific' *The Great Bear* had a wide firebox only 8ft long, though the grate area was 41.79 sq ft. In this view, note the exposed asbestos used to lag and insulate the firebox — long before the dangers this substance presents to health were appreciated.

Above: The secret of the unique success of the Churchward standard engines lay not only in their long-travel valve gear, but also in their boilers, all with Belpaire fireboxes and having a domeless barrel which tapered towards the smokebox. Several of the range of standard boilers can be seen in the row nearest the camera, in this April 20 1932 scene (left to right): Standard No. 7 ('4700' class 2—8—0s); Standard No. 1 ('Saint' and 'Hall' 4—6—0s and '2800' class 2—8—0s); Standard No. 8 ('Castle' 4—6—0s); Standard No. 1 (off No. 4950 *Patshull Hall*); and Standard No. 12 ('King' 4—6—0s). In the centre background a pair of inverted boilers are having lower steel sidesheets renewed, whilst on the right a boiler is perfectly balanced in the single sling of an overhead gantry hoist. An ashpan is lying on the floor, adjacent to the No. 12 boiler.

'KINGS' & 'CASTLES'

Above: Seen here at Swindon on July 2 1930 is a superb line-up of seven of Britain's most powerful express passenger locomotives, something never previously seen at Swindon — and it is to be doubted if it was ever seen again. The occasion was the emergence from the Works of three new engines of the second Lot, built in 1930: a fourth engine was only a month old, and the remaining 'Kings' (built in 1927-28) were probably ex-Works after being overhauled. The engines are (left to right):- Nos. 6005 *King George II,* 6008 *King James II,* 6017 *King Edward IV,* 6020 *King Henry IV* (built April 1930), 6022 *King Edward III,* 6023 *King Edward II* and 6024 *King Edward I* — the last three being brand-new. The 'Kings' were employed on the heaviest main line express duties to the end, when all 30 engines were withdrawn during 1962. The original caption reads: "A line of the new King class engines employed on the GWR leaving the running sheds at Swindon, to rush excursion trains of happy holiday makers to the seaside". However, No. 6017 was shedded at Wolverhampton and was unlikely to be used on such romantic workings!

Right: A much less-common view of the seven 'Kings', seen from the rear. The three new engines, built that month, are nearest to the camera. No. 6017 *King Edward IV* (of Wolverhampton, Stafford Road) is the 'black sheep', with a distinctly dirty cab roof: one wonders if the shed foreman and, in turn, the cleaners, got a 'rollicking' when Collett saw the photographs! Beyond the ramped coaling stage, a mineral wagon is still labelled 'LNW', seven years after the Grouping.

126

Above: The latest 'King' poses for a 'state portrait': No. 6024 *King Edward I*, together with the other three new engines, would shortly be travelling down to South Devon where all would be shedded, either at Laira or Newton Abbot, for the greater part of their lives. No. 6024 was soon to be subjected to the gruelling test of the well-known inclines between Newton Abbot and Plymouth — Dainton, Rattery and Hemerdon — where even the mighty 'Kings' were limited to 360 tons unassisted over the 1 in 37 gradients. However, in 1935 No. 6016 *King Edward V* took 11 carriages, 376 tons tare (405 tons laden), on the down 'Cornish Riviera Express' without assistance, covering the 52 miles from Exeter to Plymouth in 69½ mins — the advertised time allowance being 72 minutes! This was the heaviest recorded load ever taken without an assistant engine during the age of steam on the South Devon main line. No. 6024 is preserved at the Buckinhamshire Railway Centre.

Left, upper: The GWR missed no opportunity to publicise its new 'Castle' class engines. No. 4077 *Chepstow Castle* is pictured at Chepstow Station in July 1926, when the new Chepstow racecourse was nearing completion — the first meeting being held there the following month. The bogie brakes (originally fitted to Nos. 4073-82) have already been removed. The first eleven 'Castles', Nos. 4073-83, were all initially shedded at Old Oak Common, but *Chepstow Castle* soon moved to Newton Abbot where it spent about 30 years before finally being shedded at Bristol: it was withdrawn in 1962.

Left, lower: A line of express passenger locomotives awaiting the call at Old Oak Common on July 27 1931, in readiness for the day's holiday traffic, is led by 'Castle' No. 4009 *Shooting Star* (rebuilt from a 'Star' in April 1925), the remaining engines being a 'King' (believed to be No. 6025 *King Henry III*), a 'Star' — whose driver is kneeling on the frame platform to oil the inside motion — a 'Hall', and a 'King'.

127

Right: Having been rebuilt in 1925 from a 'Star' into a 'Castle', although retaining the name *Shooting Star*, No. 4009 experienced another transformation in 1936 when it was both renamed and renumbered. At first it carried unique number plates inscribed 'A1' to complement its new name of *Lloyds*, thereby echoing the familiar phrase 'A1 at Lloyds' — an acknowledged expression of guaranteed soundness. Additional plates with the number 100 were added above the original 'A1' plates during the following month, while the number 100 was added to the buffer beam — but on the opposite side of the coupling. '100 A1' was the highest Lloyds Register ship classification. The naming ceremony took place at Paddington on February 17 and was performed by Sir Robert Horne, Vice Chairman of the GWR in the presence of Lloyd's officials. The nameplate was surmounted by Lloyd's Coat-of-Arms, while a string of flags of the International Code, between the chimney and the cab, read 'A.1 at Lloyd's'. Despite such an assurance, No. 100 A1 suffered the dubious distinction of being the first 'Castle' to be withdrawn from service, in March 1950 — two months before the first of the final lot of 10 'Castles' was built! As *Shooting Star* its early years as a 'Castle' were spent at Laira, but from the time of its renaming it was always shedded at Old Oak Common.

Above: No. 5018 *St. Mawes Castle* is the first in a line of express passenger engines being serviced at Old Oak Common, in July 1932. This engine was often used on the 'Cheltenham Flyer', and on one celebrated occasion No. 5018 took a train of 10 carriages (340 tons) over the 77.3 miles from Swindon to Paddington in 63 minutes, reaching 82 mph at three points on the journey. Note that, compared with the earlier 'Castles', the cover over the inside cylinders is of a different pattern, somewhat similar to that on the 'Kings' (the early 'Castles' being similar to the 'Stars'). Other detail differences included a slight reduction in the grate area to provide wider water spaces: these applied to No. 5013 onwards in the series. No. 5018 led rather a roving life, commencing as a new engine (July 1932) at Old Oak Common, it was successively shedded at Wolverhampton, Gloucester and Reading, — from whence it was withdrawn in March 1964.

Left: Pictured in the works yard at Swindon in 1932 is No. 6025 *King Henry III,* after a heavy repair. This engine spent most of its life working from Old Oak Common, but had two spells in the West of England. When only two months old, it spent three months at Exeter: in 1930 Reading and Exeter or Taunton had a 'King' as stand-by engine in case of a failure on the 'Cornish Riviera Express', a provision which lasted for only a few months. From 1948-59 No. 6025 was shedded at Laira. It was one of the last four 'Kings' in service, and was withdrawn from Old Oak Common in December 1962.

Below: Gresley's superb 'A4' class 'Pacifics', introduced in September 1935, are commonly regarded as being the first streamlined locomotives to run in this country; however, it was Swindon which actually produced the first examples — in March 1935. 'Castle' No. 5005 *Manorbier Castle* and 'King' No. 6014 *King Henry VII* emerged from Swindon with bull noses, flared coverings over the cylinders and steam chests, straight splashers and nameplates, and cowlings behind the chimney and safety-valve covers, as well as wedge-fronted cabs: There was also cowling over the tops of the tenders. The result, as shown here by No. 6014, was hideous. It has been said that Collett was under pressure to streamline some engines, before the LNER 'A4s' appeared. Collett is reported to have worked out the details by sticking plasticine on a paper weight model of a 'King' on his desk! The fairings were removed piecemeal during the next few years, though No. 6014 (seen here) retained the wedge-fronted cab until withdrawal in September 1962; that on No. 5005 was replaced by a conventional cab in 1947.

DIESEL RAILCARS

Right: GWR diesel railcar No. 1 (built in 1933) was intended for use on local passenger services, and worked on the main line between Slough and Reading. It is seen here at West Drayton & Yiewsley, on February 2 1934. There was accommodation for 69 passengers in two compartments, between which was a centre entrance vestibule, while luggage was carried in the larger of the two end driving compartments. The seats were arranged back-to-back on each side of an off-centre gangway, with three seats on one side and two on the other. The power was supplied by a single AEC diesel engine of 130 bhp and transmitted to the wheels through a drive enclosed in the axle boxes on the ends of the axle. Note the fine collection of platform slot machines and the 'Wait here for Rail Car' notice.

Above: Originally entitled: "A Railway Contrast. The Great Western Railway's new streamlined railcar alongside a West of England Express as they speed across Maidenhead Bridge", this is actually a composite picture formed from two photographs — the join being made down the right-hand edge of the sleepers of the track on which the railcar is travelling. The locomotive on the express is a 'Saint' 4—6—0 one of 13 engines which commenced their existence as 'Atlantic' 4—4—2 s, and which were rebuilt during 1912-13, when the curved drop-ends were fitted to the platforms (as in the 'Saint' and 'Court' series) though they retained lever reverse.

Below, left: The next three diesel railcars (Nos. 2-4) were designed for express services, with a maximum speed of 75-80 mph, compared with No. 1's top speed of 60 mph. Two 130 bhp engines were employed, each mounted along one side of the frames. One engine drove two axles of one bogie through a Wilson pre-selector epicyclic gearbox, a reversing box and two sets of worm gearing; the engine on the other side driving directly (without the epicyclic gearbox) on one axle of the other bogie. The bodies were again built by Park Royal Coachworks Ltd., but the gangways were central with two seats on each side, with tables between the seats. The two compartments seated 40 passengers, while a third compartment contained a buffet with a further four seats and there were two small lavatory cubicles — in contrast to No. 1 which was 'dry'! These buffet railcars were used on a Cardiff and Birmingham express service, stopping only at Newport and Gloucester, though No. 2 was at first used on an experimental service between Oxford and Hereford. One of the new railcars is seen here under construction at Park Royal Coachworks on June 25 1934. Like No. 1, Nos. 2-4 had special buffers and concealed drawgear, normally hidden by a rectangular panel. Whereas the driver's doors on No. 1 were curved and could only be entered by clambering over the streamlined valances, the later cars' doors were flat and situated at the sides of the cabs. Another visible difference was that No. 1 proudly bore the GWR Coat-of-Arms, front and rear, whereas Nos. 2-4 displayed the new 'roundel'.

Above, right: Railcars Nos. 5-16 were introduced during 1935/36, the bodies being built by the Gloucester Railway Carriage & Wagon Co. Ltd. Generally similar to No. 1 in accommodation (though Nos. 10-12 seated only 63 passengers, due to the provision of a lavatory compartment), they had twin 130 bhp engines as on the three express railcars Nos. 2-4. An innovation was the provision of sliding doors, those on Nos. 1-4 having been of the normal hinged type. No. 11 is seen at AEC's works at Southall, prior to delivery to the GWR, on January 13 1936.

Above: As shown here on car No. 11, the sides of the streamlined railcars were carried down to within about 12 inches of rail level, totally enclosing the underframe, although several sections were removable for access to the engines and bogies. Problems with overheating led to the cars running with the sections of the valance removed from the driving side of each bogie: this was done on No. 2 prior to the special press run from Birmingham to Cardiff on July 6 1934, though it ran with all panels in place on the Oxford and Hereford service. Note the whitewall tyres.

ALTHOUGH the former London & Northern Western Railway, self-styled the 'Premier Line', was wont to claim that it was 'the oldest passenger carrying line in existence' (on the strength of the Liverpool & Manchester Railway's opening in 1830), only the GWR achieved the distinction of celebrating its centenary.

Held in 1935, the Centenary celebrations were a 'cheat' to some extent, for this was the centenary of the Royal Assent to the Great Western Bill of August 31 1835 and not of the actual opening of the first section of its line, from Paddington to Maidenhead, which did not take place until May 31 1838. The opening had been the occasion for one of the Bristol Directors, T.R. Guppy, to distinguish himself by walking along the tops of the carriages from one end of the train to the other while it was going at full speed: doubtless this occurred on the return journey after the luncheon and the usual complement of toasts!

The Royal Assent had not been obtained without considerable opposition, some of the fiercest being from the Provost and Fellows of Eton College, who were successful in obtaining provisions in the Bill which precluded the Directors from "constructing any Station or Depot within three miles of Eton College without the consent of the Provost and Fellows of that Establishment". However, the GWR was not precluded from arranging for its trains to stop at Slough and the Directors promised: "The trains will of course convey any passengers who may be desirous of travelling to and from the neighbourhood of Slough, and the Directors can only regret that they are not at liberty to provide the ordinary conveniences of a Station for Persons waiting there to be received on the Railway".

The Provost and Fellows, furious at this attack on the morals of their school, applied in vain for an injunction to prevent such action. However, the Eton masters were not long in recognising the advantages of the railway, for within a month of their defeat — and while an appeal was still pending — they asked the GWR to provide a special train to take the boys up to town for the Coronation on June 28 1838. The GWR, doubtless not wishing to bear malice — and, no doubt, also mindful of the revenue — duly provided the train!

The Centenary was marked on August 31, 1935 by a great celebration in Bristol, where the Company had its birth. The celebration lunch, in

THE GWR CENTENARY

Above: The GWR Centenary was marked by the introduction of a new high-speed 'Bristolian' express, and on the Centenary Day (August 31) the special express conveying the London party to Bristol left Paddington at 10.00am, the time fixed for the new high-speed service. There could be no question as to which locomotive would be given the honour of hauling the special train on this unique occasion: carrying the official reporting number '010' — the only time this was ever used — No. 6000 *King George V,* complete with the bell which was the legacy of its triumphant American visit in 1927, takes the Centenary train out of Paddington. One doubts if Brunel would have fully approved of this scene with its multiple track layout all on the 'narrow gauge' — but he would surely have recognised that the GWR was still "the finest work in England". The original Topical Press caption for this photograph stated: "this express is likely to attain 100 miles per hour on the run from Paddington" — which was highly unlikely on a two-hour schedule! The redoubtable C.J. Allen, writing in his monthly 'British Locomotive Practice and Performance' in the *Railway Magazine,* described the running as devoid of note". On the return journey, Mr. Allen had been expecting a good run: "It had been freely rumoured that a new 'record of records' was to be attempted and I was looking forward to run up in roughly 90 mins, in the proportion of about 37 min to Swindon and 53 min from Swindon, passed at full speed to Paddington, which would roughly have equalled the Cheltenham Flyer times of June 6 1932. But it was not to be; and strict adherence to schedule was the order of the day ..." Indeed, on the return journey, when the train consisted of six of the Super Saloons built for the Ocean Liner Specials from Plymouth, and a kitchen car, on a 105-minute schedule via the Badminton line the train was 1½ minutes late at Southall, which resulted in a tremendous acceleration to 88 mph between Acton and Old Oak Common to ensure an arrival 'on time' at Paddington. The footplatemen were Driver Sparrow and Fireman Sims, both of Old Oak Common, and the seven-coach train weighed 251 tons (tare) and 265 tons (gross). The new 'Bristolian' was booked to run from Paddington to Bristol in 105 minutes, requiring a start-to-stop average speed 67.6 mph. The 'Cornish Riviera Express' still remained as the GWR's most prestigious express however, and new carriages were provided for its patrons during the centenary year. Comprised of 13 vehicles, the new trains seated 84 first class, 336 third class and 88 dining passengers within a total weight of around 420 tons tare. The new coaches were 60ft long and at 9ft 7in wide were the widest passenger vehicles at work in the country.

Below: The Centenary celebrations of 1935 also included the appearance of the replica *North Star* and train on a short length of broad gauge track at Maidenhead (though not, alas, on genuine 'baulk road') to enable the arrival of the GWR's first train to be re-enacted. This *North Star*, first seen ten years earlier at the Stockton & Darlington Centenary, was not a working locomotive, as indicated by the presence of a small locomotive at the rear of the train. This was No. 1, the first diesel shunter to be purchased by the GWR, a little-known engine built by John Fowler & Co. (Leeds) Ltd in 1935 and sold out of service in March 1940. This is an extremely rare photograph of this engine actually at work, and is made all the more interesting in that No. 1 is running on standard gauge metals to propel the broad gauge replica train — the mixed gauge track is visible beneath *North Star's* bufferbeam. Commenting on the Centenary, *The Railway Gazette* said: "Never before in the history of the railways of Great Britain — the birthplace of this means of locomotion — has a main line railway company attained to the dignity of a full hundred years of corporate life. There are, of course, older railways than the GWR, but the process of amalgamation (almost as ancient as railways themselves) has always resulted in a loss of identity long before ten decades of life were run. Nor is the GWR record in this respect likely to be challenged within living memory, as the Railways Act of 1921 left only the GWR of all the main line companies to continue operating under the original charter. In its long life under the familiar title the GWR has deservedly gathered a wide circle of friends, and Lord Greenwood expressed this sentiment happily in a letter which Sir Robert Horne quoted at Bristol on Saturday when he said: 'All England seems to have a friendly family feeling for the Great Western'."

In a special centenary issue of 'The Railway Gazette', GWR General Manager James Milne said in his Foreword: "Within the century the Great Western Railway has grown from 116 miles of single track to 9,075; its capital expenditure has risen from £2,000,000 to over £183,000,000; and it has conveyed over 171 million passengers in a year, and more than 83 million tons of merchandise and mineral traffic, and could easily surpass these figures should occasion demand."

The GWR always tried to remain in the forefront in all areas of its operations, from locomotives to public facilities, and a good 'off-beat' example of imaginative progress, was reported in the October 1935 issue of 'The Railway Magazine'. The GWR announced that: "the first quick lunch and snack bar for passengers at a railway station has just been opened on Number 1 platform at Paddington. The bar provides seating accommodation on tall green-topped chromium plated stools for 27 persons. Under the counter are recesses for hats, newspapers or ladies handbags. All the service is from the inside by chefs dressed in white." The provision of 'fast food' in 1935 epitomised the forward thinking and innovative nature of the GWR which appealed so strongly to its admirers — and which so irritated its competitors!

the Great Hall of Bristol University, was attended by the Directors who were conveyed from Paddington in a special express. The Lord Mayor of Bristol and other civic dignitaries, together with representatives of the commercial and industrial interests of the city and district, were the guests of the Company at this lunch.

The Centenary celebrations culminated in the Banquet held at the Grosvenor House, London, on October 30, at which the Prince of Wales proposed the toast of the "Great Western Railway Company". During his speech, he said: "I wish to pay my tribute to all that the Great Western Railway has done for the West Country during the century of its existence. Speed, comfort, convenience, flexibility, have all been keynotes of your administration. It can never be said, that the Great Western Railway has not moved with the times. It is a fact that your company was the first railway company to establish, a few years ago, a regular daily air service. You have held the balance fairly between competing interests. You have discharged your duty to the public with loyalty. You are a venerable, honourable, institution in our native land".

THE magazine 'Picture Post', which disappeared from the news stands in 1957, was very much a victim of the television age. Before the television camera usurped its role, the magazine had specialised in high quality, imaginative photo-journalism and a 'Picture Post' story would cover perhaps eight pages, and always featured photographs which captured the very essence of the subject, in addition to just its physical appearance. In April 1942, 'Picture Post' photographer Bert Hardy visited Paddington station to photograph the GWR at war, and the resulting story,

WARTIME TERMINUS

'Wartime Terminus' appeared in the issue published on May 23 1942. A selection of Mr. Hardy's photographs are reproduced here, and we have retained that original headline as a tribute both to 'Picture Post's' highly creative approach and the undoubted skill of Bert Hardy. In discussing the relative merits of 'Castles' or 'Kings', or researching the finer detail of carriage liveries and construction, it is easy to forget that the railways

were both the creation and servant of the people who operated and used them — and these powerful pictures put that consideration into very sharp focus indeed. In the pre-Nationalisation years of limited car ownership, most people travelling any distance in this country used the train, and in wartime the thousands of arrivals and departures occurring on the platforms of a large railway station were particularly emotional.

Above, left: Women at War I: "The train now arriving at platform 1 . . .". The smooth running of a major terminus like Paddington, especially in wartime, depended as much on the 'white collar' staff as it did on the shunters, footplatemen and platform staff. With just a single lamp to assist her, the Paddington station announcer prepares to send another important message echoing around Brunel's lofty train shed, in April 1942.

Above, right: Women at War II: a group of lady porters handle mail at Paddington in April 1942, assisted by an elderly porter who may have been one of many GWR company servants who came out of retirement to help the national effort. The station master still wears his immaculate top hat, war or no war!

Facing page, top: 'Western approaches' was a familiar war-time description of the Atlantic Ocean to the south west of Britain, but it applied equally well to the approaches to Paddington, as seen here in April 1942. Many carriages are painted all-over brown, reverting to the livery used prior to 1864 and between 1908 and 1912. Two of the '6100' class 2—6—2Ts, built between 1931 and 1935 to replace the '2221' class 4—4—2Ts and '3600' class 2—4—2Ts on the London suburban services, are to be seen. On the left, No. 6126 heads an outward-bound train over the electrified lines shared with the London Underground from what was formerly Bishop's Road station, while No. 6131 stands by a typical GWR water tank, waiting to run back into the station.

Right: "Shine through the gloom". A shaft of sunshine pierces the darkness and smoke at Paddington to strike the cab side of No. 4979 *Wootton Hall* (of Tyseley) as the driver smiles down at the small girl who appears rather overwhelmed at being so near a large locomotive. In common with all GWR engines having cabs of this design, the glass has been removed from the side windows and replaced by steel sheeting. This was done for Air Raid Precaution purposes, though only the GWR — ever safety-conscious — appears to have taken such action. The war took a terrible toll on the railways, with much essential maintenance being missed in the desperate attempt to keep trains moving, and keep the enemy at bay. Locomotive cleaning was a very early casualty and GWR locomotives, once so pristine, became inevitably grimy and unkempt. The shaft of sunlight striking *Wootton Hall* reveals the wheels and siderods to be covered in dirt and grease — a far cry indeed from the gleaming image of the 1930s, as illustrated on page 104, for example.

Most of the pictures in this section feature GWR hardware in only hazy or peripheral detail — yet they are undoubtedly railway photographs of the highest quality, providing evocative reflections of the GWR hard at work during a period of extreme national peril.

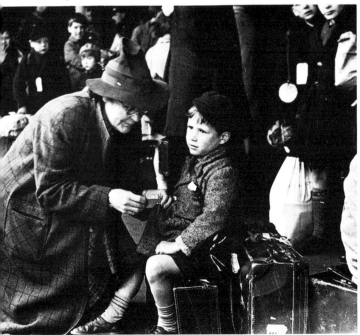

Left: The early weeks of the war witnessed the evacuation of many thousands of children from London to the greater safety of other areas — mostly in the West Country. The scale of the operation was huge: 12 coach trains seating 800 passengers were used, no less than 50 train-sets being required to carry through the programme. The evacuation was spread over four days and the special timetable provided for the timing of 64 trains each day, 60 of which ran from Ealing Broadway which was closed to ordinary passengers between 8.00 am and 5.30 pm on those days. The special trains were planned to leave at 9-minute intervals throughout the period 8.30 am to 5.30 pm. The number of trains actually run depended on each day's requirements, and varied from 58 trains, with 44,032 passengers, on the first day, to 28 trains which carried 17,796 passengers on the final day. The down relief line was devoted entirely to these trains, all other traffic running over the main lines: local trains were restricted to one per hour and the main line service was greatly reduced — only 13 trains leaving Paddington between 8.30 am and 5.30 pm. However, many of the children were unhappy away from home, living with strangers, and this was the 'Phoney War' — the threatened air raids did not come and by January 1940 nearly one million had returned home to the cities. Then the Luftwaffe's bombers did arrive, and a second evacuation began. In April 1942, this young man looks particularly bewildered and dejected, accompanied by battered suitcases, and with his name and other personal details written on a luggage label as he is evacuated from the capital. The original 'Picture Post' caption added that: ". . . children have been leaving London for months regularly under this trickle system."

FORCES personnel frequently outnumbered civilians at Paddington during the years 1939-45, and there were frequent moments of joy and sadness as families were either reunited or separated with the ebb and flow of military fortunes in the war, whose end at this point was three years distant.

Left: "We few, we happy few . . ." *(Shakespeare, King Henry V).*

Facing page: "And think of nought, save where you are . . ." *(Shakespeare, Sonnets).* **A tearful farewell as a train pulls out of Paddington, leaving those at home to worry and hope.**

Right: A sad and anguished moment as a family is parted at Paddington in April 1942.

Right: "The Yanks are coming, the Yanks are here." The Second World War witnessed the arrival in Britain not only of 'Uncle Sam's' troops and airmen, but also his locomotives, as illustrated here at Paddington in January 1943. A total of 390 American-built 'S160' class 2—8—0s built in readiness for use on the continent after the liberation, spent several months working in this country prior to D Day. They appeared on GWR metals and No. 1604, pictured here, was ceremonially handed over at Paddington in January 1943, suitably adorned with the 'Union Jack' and the 'Stars and Stripes'. These locomotives were very different in outline from any contemporary British locomotives; they pulled well and steamed well but British crews found their large cabs to be very draughty. Note the four holes on the bufferbeam indicating the removal of the US 'buckeye' coupling in favour of the more primitive British drawhook and screw shackle.

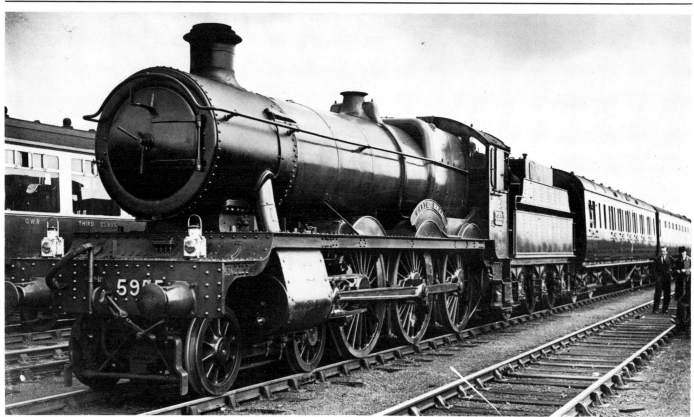

Above: No. 5955 *Garth Hall*, the first GWR passenger locomotive modified for oil burning, pictured on August 8 1946. A further ten 'Halls' were similarly converted during April and May 1947, while five 'Castles' were altered to burn oil between October 1946 and January 1947. *Garth Hall* initially retained its original number, but the 'Halls' were later temporarily renumbered into a 39xx series (the former 49xx becoming Nos. 3900-4, and those from the 59xx and 69xx series becoming Nos. 3950-55. Similarly, the oil-burning 2—8—0s were renumbered into the 48xx series (thus requiring the little '4800' class 0—4—2Ts to become Nos. 1400-74), but the 'Castles' were never renumbered. Note here the war-time livery of overall black (carried by all except the 'Stars', 'Castles' and 'Kings') has given place to the traditional Brunswick green, but without any lining.

POST-WAR MOTIVE POWER

Left: The fireman in the cab of *Garth Hall*, photographed on August 8 1946 during a trial run from Paddington: note the 'Burner Steam Pressure' gauge fitted below the boiler pressure gauge which is reading slightly less than 240 psi. The valve wheels controlled the flow of oil to the burners in the firebox. The water gauge glass shows the boiler to be two-thirds full and note the bracket on its left, on which the gauge lamp (sitting on the shelf over the firehole door) was mounted. Although it had been intended that Cornwall should be the sphere of operation for the oil-burning passenger engines, they worked mainly between Paddington, Bristol and Plymouth, while the oil-burning 2—8—0s worked from Llanelly and Severn Tunnel Junction to Plymouth, Bristol and London.

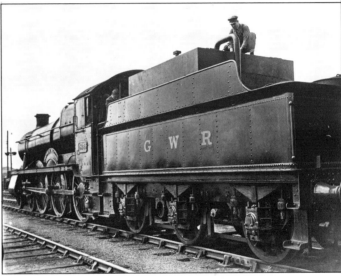

Above: *Garth Hall* and the first 'Castle' to be converted to oil burning (No. 5901 *Cleeve Abbey*) were given low-sided 3,500 gallon tenders, as shown here, but the other converted 'Halls' and 'Castles' had the usual high-sided 4,000 gallon type. The pre-war GWR 'roundel' was replaced by the initials GWR on No. 5995's tender, but the post-war standard 'G' and 'W' on either side of the Coat-of-Arms was later applied. Note the sliding steel shutters on the cab window: these were similar to those fitted since the 1930s to the GWR's larger tank engines. The oil burning trials were carried out in conjunction with the Anglo-Iranian Oil Company, and the original caption to this picture said: "Mr. Leonard Chillingsworth who will be the fireman of the oil-burning loco, attends to the filling taps on the oil container". No. 5955, subsequently returned to coal firing and its original number, was eventually withdrawn from service in April 1965 from Bristol Barrow Road shed and scrapped.

DURING the winter of 1945 the supply of locomotive coal became a serious problem (due to heavy-handed and damaging Government control of all coal supplies) and the GWR decided to equip a number of locomotives for oil firing. Initially, 18 heavy mineral engines of the '2800' class 2-8-0s were scheduled for conversion, being intended for working through the South Wales area. This was an ironic situation, as this was the area which produced the best locomotive coal; however, this fuel was being exported and the local railways were attempting, rather unsuccessfully, to run on imported American coal which was of very inferior quality!

The following year a further experiment commenced, when it was decided to make Cornwall an oil-fired area to the exclusion of all coal-burning locomotives — though one could hardly describe this as the first 'smokeless zone'! Prior to the war, serious examination had been given to the possibility of electrifying the lines in the West of England, due to the cost of transporting locomotive coal and the choice of Cornwall for an oil-firing area was partly based on the same reasoning. However, it was also because the constant succession of gradients and an overall speed limit of 60 mph resulted in widely varying demands being made upon the boiler, and fuel consumption was consequently heavy.

It was intended that a number of 'Hall' and 'Castle' 4-6-0s should be converted, and 11 of the former and five of the latter were converted for oil-burning during 1946-47. However, due to yet further interference and mismanagement by the Government, the scheme was doomed to failure. The Ministry of Transport ordered the conversion of several hundred engines of the 'Big Four' Companies, but hardly had this work (which included the installing of numerous oil storage tanks at engine sheds) commenced, when it was discovered that this country lacked the foreign currency to pay for the oil! The highly sensible and economically sound GWR perished in the fiasco, for

Nationalisation followed soon after, on January 1, 1948.

IN 1946 the GWR made locomotive history when an order was placed for a gas turbine locomotive from the Swiss firm of Brown-Boveri, based upon that firm's original turbine locomotive which had been in service in Switzerland since September 1941. It was to be the third example in the world; an American-built locomotive for the Union Pacific Railroad entered service a few months earlier than the example ordered by the GWR.

A gas turbine works in similar style to a jet engine, by inhaling large quantities of air into a compressor, and heating this air by passing it through a combustion chamber in which fuel oil is burned, the air then emerging from the chamber at high velocity to drive a turbine. The turbine drives an electric generator through gearing, and the current produced drives traction motors: in the case of the GWR locomotive there were four such motors, two in each bogie — the centre wheels unpowered; it was thus of the A-1-A+A-1-A arrangement.

Heavy fuel oil (sufficient for 250 miles of running), lubricating oil and water were carried partially in the roof and partially in the middle portion of the main frames. An auxiliary diesel-generator was placed at one end of the power unit, in company with the train heating boiler and one of the traction motor fans; at the other end were the exhaust-compressor set for the brakes (which were duplicated for electrical and mechanical operation) together with the other fan. The auxiliary generator provided electric current for all the auxiliaries and could supply current to two of the four traction motors for working the locomotive from the running sheds to the station. The steam heating boiler was automatically fired with oil.

The GWR locomotive could be driven from either end, both cabs being fitted with remote controls for the gas turbine power unit, the diesel generator set and the auxiliary apparatus. Capable of a maximum speed of 90 mph, the locomotive was 63ft long and weighed 115 tons. Long before the locomotive was delivered, the GWR had ceased to exist, and it was British Railways (Western Region) which took delivery, early in 1950. Prior to entering service on May 9, it worked a number of trial trips during which, as might have been expected with such a revolutionary new design, some teething troubles were encountered, including damage to the turbine. After working a number of passenger turns between Swindon and Paddington, it entered service on express trains between Paddington and Plymouth and Bristol.

Above: The steam age meets the jet age on Brunel's 'home ground' — No. 18000, painted in impressive black and silver livery, stands at Paddington on May 10 1950, its first appearance at Brunel's great station. Its regular working was the 9.15am Paddington-Bristol and the 4.15pm Bristol-Paddington, though when new it also appeared on the 'Cornish Riviera Express' on several occasions. It was found to consume almost as much fuel when idling or when running under reduced power as under full load, and, contrary to expectations, gave no significant advantage over diesel-electric locomotives. Withdrawn in December 1960 after ten years of intermittent service, No. 18000 became the property of the Swiss Railways, who used it as a mobile laboratory, and it is now preserved at the Brown-Boveri Works, Geneva.

Left: A second gas turbine locomotive was ordered from Metropolitan-Vickers Electrical Company Ltd. who were also the designers. Financial and technical responsibility for the project were shared by the makers and British Railways. No. 18100 was delivered to Swindon on December 16 1951 and taken into stock in April 1952. Although similar to the earlier engine in the general arrangement of the plant and control equipment, all three axles on both bogies had driving motors. It was slightly longer (66ft 9ins) and quite a few tons heavier, weighing 129 tons, and was capable of the same maximum speed of 90mph. It was the most powerful passenger engine on British Railways — the most powerful locomotive being the famous LNER 'Beyer-Garratt'. No. 18100 is seen here on display at Paddington station in April 1952: one would hope that Brunel would have admired and approved of it! No. 18100 was used on similar duties to No. 18000 when that engine was new, but it had a short working life. It was withdrawn in January 1958 and was then converted by the makers into another experimental locomotive — a 25kv electric locomotive numbered E1000 (later E2001). Used for crew training in the early days of the LMR main line electrification, it was not withdrawn until April 1968. However, its usefulness was not over, as it was sent to Akeman Street (on the former GCR line from Ashendon Junction to Grendon Junction) and used in experiments to determine the effect of cross winds on the pantograph. Towed to the Rugby Locomotive Testing Station in May 1972, the locomotive was sold for scrap to Cashmore's of Great Bridge in January 1973 — an ignoble end for a most adventurous project.

Left: A view inside the No. 2 end drivers cab of No. 18100, which must have been a very different world from the footplates of the Swindon-built steam locomotives on which engine crews mainly worked.

Above: A 'works' view of the gas turbine power plant fitted to No. 18100: it was in keeping with the GWRs innovative tradition that this 'jet age' traction was being experimented with even before the last 'Castle' 4—6—0s were run-in, and a full decade before standard gauge steam construction ended!

WESTERN REGION

AT midnight on December 31, 1947, the railway of Isambard Kingdom Brunel and Sir Daniel Gooch, G.J. Churchward, Viscount Churchill, Sir Felix J. Pole and a host of other famous names, the organisation known to many as 'God's Wonderful Railway' came to an end of a life which had lasted for no less than 112 years. Although this was a far more traumatic event than the ending of the broad gauge on May 20, 1892, the visible effects were far less noticeable. At 11.50pm the last GWR train left Paddington, this being the overnight service to Plymouth via Bristol (reminiscent of Brunel and those days when GWR had also meant 'Great Way Round') hauled by No. 5037 *Monmouth Castle* of Old Oak Common shed. At 12.05am, No. 5032 *Usk Castle,* a Shrewsbury (Salop) engine left at the head of the overnight train to Birkenhead, the first train to leave Paddington under British Railways (Western Region) ownership.

A strong contrast in WR operations of 1952:

Right, upper: King George Vi died in February 1952 and Paddington was once again the departure point for a royal funeral train. The engine for the royal funeral train, No. 4082 *Windsor Castle,* stands in Paddington station, on February 23 1952, carrying the draped Coat-of-Arms and the special headlamp code. In contrast to the funeral trains for the two previous monarchs, only the extra-large lamp on the smokebox door was surmounted by a crown — the former practice having been to have two such lamps, one over each buffer. As with previous royal funerals, the train started from platform 8. The locomotive was not the genuine No. 4082 (built 1924) which had shortly beforehand been taken into Swindon, for overhaul. In its place was No. 7013 *Bristol Castle,* with which it permanently exchanged identities. The original *Windsor Castle,* as No. 7013, was rebuilt with a double chimney in May 1958 and was not withdrawn until February 1965, after 41 years of life: the 'new' No. 4082, built in July 1948, lasted only until September 1964 — a mere 16 years.

Right, below: Railways have frequently featured in cinema feature films, but one of the most affectionately remembered productions is 'The Titfield Thunderbolt', made by Ealing Studios in 1952. Telling the story of how a local community acquired and operated its own branch line in the face of closure by British Railways, the film unintentionally foretold the future development of standard gauge steam preservation. The film was shot at Monckton Combe station, on the abandoned Camerton-Limpley Stoke branch in Somerset, which closed to passengers in 1925 and goods in 1951. Above, left: '4800' class 0—4—2T No. 1401 bears down on actor Hugh Griffiths and a motor lorry in the film's famous road-rail confrontation on a level crossing. Certainly a dramatic photograph! There were 75 auto-fitted engines of this class built during the 1930s, a further 20 engines in the 58xx series being non-fitted. They became synonymous with the typical

GWR branch line train consisting of one of these engines attached to one or two auto-trailers. However, they were also used on some main line auto-train workings, including an early morning return trip between Newton Abbot and Totnes (which took them up over Dainton bank) and they were quite capable of reaching 70 mph! No. 1401, the second of the class to be built (in August 1932), led a wandering life: having been sent when new to Cheltenham, by 1938 it was at Leamington; in 1947 it was working from Croes Newydd shed (Wrexham), whilst at the time the film was made it was allocated to Banbury. It was withdrawn in January 1958 from Cheltenham, its original shed.

Left, upper: Yet another new royal connection for the 'Royal Road' on January 29 1952 was the granting of the name 'The Royal Duchy' to the 1.30pm Paddington-Penzance and the 11.30am Penzance-Paddington trains. It is interesting to recall that among the names suggested in 1904 for what became the 'Cornish Riviera Express' had been the 'Royal Duchy Express'. However, before such a name could be bestowed, permission had to be obtained from Buckingham Palace. The GWR was still very much alive in spirit, so that it was only to be expected that No. 6000 *King George V* would be in charge of the 1.30pm from Paddington on the occasion of its first journey as 'The Royal Duchy' on January 29 1952. Immaculate and a credit to Old Oak Common's cleaners, No. 6000 awaits departure at Paddington with its driver and fireman in high spirits. The distinctive headboard incorporated the arms of the Duchy of Cornwall, reviving memories of the time when 'Bulldog' class 4—4—0 No. 3351 *One and All* (the motto of the Royal Duchy) carried the arms of the Duchy of Cornwall in brass above the combined name and number plates on the cab sides. Either the old Great Western Railway or the new Western Region was wrong, as the 'Bulldog's' crest had included a crown above the shield!

Left, lower: The GWR's famous chocolate and cream carriage livery made an unexpected and most welcome reappearance on a number of named trains during 1956: there were those who maintained that the considerable increase of named trains on the Western Region at this time was due solely to the desire to paint as many carriages as possible in the old livery! The first three trains to be thus distinguished were the 'Cornish Riviera Express', the 'Torbay Express' and 'The Bristolian'. Specially designed head-boards were provided for the locomotives working these trains, and that for 'The Bristolian' incorporated the Coats-of-Arms of the City of London and of the City and County of Bristol — which had of course comprised the Coat-of-Arms of the former Great Western Railway! In true GWR fashion, 'Castle' No. 5044 *Earl of Dunraven* takes 'The Bristolian' out of Paddington in fine style on June 11 1956. This engine was built in March 1936, when it was named *Beverston Castle*: it was renamed *Earl of Dunraven* in September 1937. The change of name was due to the 'Earl' names being transferred from the double-framed 4—4—0s which had been produced by marrying 'Duke' class boilers and 'Bulldog' class frames — a hybrid widely known in later years as 'Dukedog'. No. 5044's original name, *Beverston Castle,* was later given to No. 5068 built in June 1938. After spending most of its life working from Old Oak Common, No. 5044 was withdrawn from Cardiff, Canton in September 1962. The train identification or 'reporting' numbers, No. 116 in this instance, were first introduced by the GWR in the summer of 1934 purely for Saturday trains. It was hoped that this would minimise delays and assist in the handling of trains during the height of the holiday season. Reintroduced for the 1946 summer season, the scheme covered all weekday trains in some instances, many more trains being numbered than in pre-war days. That this system, modified by the use of a letter and figures, is still in use today is proof of the value of the original conception.

Below: Journey's end. Two names may be said to epitomise the unique characteristics and excellence of the Great Western Railway. Much of its system was surveyed and engineered by the genius and abilities of Isambard Kingdom Brunel, while another genius, George Jackson Churchward, was responsible for its revolutionary range of standard locomotives. In this evocative scene, the legacies of both great men are brought together: one of Churchward's magnificent 'Saint' class 4—6—0s, No. 2952 *Twineham Court,* stands against the bufferstops beneath the equally magnificent iron scrollwork in Brunel's Paddington Station — the 'Gateway to the West'.

Above: At the turn of the century, the memory of former senior Officers of the Company had been honoured by their names being carried on some of the latest express passenger engines, but in the latter days of the GWR only Isambard Kingdom Brunel and Sir Daniel Gooch were commemorated (by 'Castles' Nos. 5069 and 5070). However, the Western Region paid a very belated tribute to G.J. Churchward, the architect of GWR locomotive practice in this century and one of the outstanding locomotive engineers of all time, who was also the first Mayor of the Borough of Swindon. BR-built 'Castle' class locomotive No. 7017 was named *G.J. Churchward* at a special ceremony held at Paddington Station on October 29 1948, the ceremony being performed by Capt. E. William Gregson, RNR, President of the Institute of Mechanical Engineers. No. 7017 was shedded at Old Oak Common throughout its relatively short life: it was withdrawn in February 1963. It is interesting to note that although 20 out of the 30 'Castles' built by British Railways were rebuilt with double chimneys (66 members of the class ended their lives in this condition) neither No. 7017 *G.J. Churchward* or No. 7037 *Swindon* were among them.